The Day's Mischief

Lesley Storm

A Samuel French Acting Edition

SAMUELFRENCH.COM
SAMUELFRENCH-LONDON.CO.UK

Copyright © 1952 by Lesley Storm
All Rights Reserved

THE DAY'S MISCHIEF is fully protected under the copyright laws of the United States of America, the British Commonwealth, including Canada, and all other countries of the Copyright Union. All rights, including professional and amateur stage productions, recitation, lecturing, public reading, motion picture, radio broadcasting, television and the rights of translation into foreign languages are strictly reserved.

ISBN 978-0-573-01089-7

www.SamuelFrench.com
www.SamuelFrench-London.co.uk

For Production Enquiries

United States and Canada
Info@SamuelFrench.com
1-866-598-8449

United Kingdom and Europe
Plays@SamuelFrench-London.co.uk
020-7255-4302

Each title is subject to availability from Samuel French, depending upon country of performance. Please be aware that *THE DAY'S MISCHIEF* may not be licensed by Samuel French in your territory. Professional and amateur producers should contact the nearest Samuel French office or licensing partner to verify availability.

CAUTION: Professional and amateur producers are hereby warned that *THE DAY'S MISCHIEF* is subject to a licensing fee. Publication of this play(s) does not imply availability for performance. Both amateurs and professionals considering a production are strongly advised to apply to Samuel French before starting rehearsals, advertising, or booking a theatre. A licensing fee must be paid whether the title(s) is presented for charity or gain and whether or not admission is charged. Professional/Stock licensing fees are quoted upon application to Samuel French.

No one shall make any changes in this title(s) for the purpose of production. No part of this book may be reproduced, stored in a retrieval system, or transmitted in any form, by any means, now known or yet to be invented, including mechanical, electronic, photocopying, recording, videotaping, or otherwise, without the prior written permission of the publisher. No one shall upload this title(s), or part of this title(s), to any social media websites.

For all enquiries regarding motion picture, television, and other media rights, please contact Samuel French.

Please refer to page 71 for further copyright information.

THE DAY'S MISCHIEF

Produced at The Duke of York's Theatre, London, on December 11th, 1951, with the following cast of characters:

(in the order of their appearance)

STEPHEN BARLOW	*Ian Hunter*
LAURA VINING	*Muriel Pavlow*
GRACE BARLOW	*Catherine Lacey*
MRS USHER	*Marjorie Manning*
HENRY VINING	*Walter Fitzgerald*
EVELYN VINING	*Beatrix Lehmann*
VI VINING	*Nuna Davey*
SALLY	*Betty Blackler*
PHOEBE	*Barbara Fletcher*
MISS FABER	*Mavis Walker*

The Play produced by NORMAN MARSHALL

SYNOPSIS OF SCENES

ACT I
SCENE 1 The sitting-room of the Barlows' house. Evening
SCENE 2 The same. Two hours later
SCENE 3 The living-room of the Vinings' house. Three days later

ACT II
SCENE 1 The sitting-room of the Barlows' house. Ten minutes later
SCENE 2 The living-room of the Vinings' house. Three hours later

THE DAY'S MISCHIEF

ACT I

Scene 1

Scene.—*The sitting-room of the* Barlows' *house in Rudford, a provincial English town.*

The room reflects the taste of a man of considerable scholarship on a salary of about one thousand pounds a year. There are rows of books on either side of the door, which is in the back wall, and some good pieces of antique furniture, well cared for—notably a desk which fills the bay window on the L., *a settee near the fireplace,* R., *with a small table behind it, an easy chair down* R. *with a small table and reading lamp near it, and a console table down* L. *with a telephone.* Mrs Barlow *collects Bristol glass and china, and there is evidence of this among the ornaments. One or two good pictures and etchings of Oxford hang on the walls.*

(*See the Ground Plan at the end of the Play.*)

When the Curtain *rises, a folding card table stands down* L.C., *and sitting opposite to each other, on light folding chairs, are* Stephen Barlow, R. *of the table, and* Laura Vining, L. *of it. There is a book on the floor by* Laura's *left foot, also her school satchel. Each has an open exercise book, a pencil and some slim school books on the table.* Stephen *is a good-looking and attractive man in his early forties ; an Oxford graduate, he is classics master at the new large mixed County School, which is Rudford's pride.* Laura *is a shy, sensitive and attractive young girl of seventeen. The vases are filled with spring flowers from the garden.* Stephen *closes a text-book with an air of finality and, picking up all but the exercise books, rises.*

Stephen. Well, there we are. I should say you've had about enough for one evening.

Laura (*softly*). It's hopeless. I'm so sorry.

Stephen. Not exactly hopeless—difficult. You may get through with luck. If you can spare a few evenings next week we'll see what we can do.

Laura. It's very kind of you to trouble.

Stephen. Not at all. You work well, you deserve to pass. If you don't you'll have another chance in the autumn.

Laura. I'm getting so old.

Stephen (*crossing to the desk*). You'll probably find several other old ladies of seventeen in the same predicament. (*He puts down the books.*)

(LAURA *picks up the book from the floor and the exercise books on the table and packs her satchel.*)

Your grounding has been bad. You must have been going on for years without knowing the rudiments. One's knowledge has to be built from the foundations. I don't think you know the grammar.

LAURA. No, I don't.

STEPHEN. It's a serious reflection on this super-school of ours. (*He crosses to the fireplace.*)

LAURA. It wasn't the school—it was my father.

STEPHEN. Did he teach you in the beginning?

LAURA. Yes—but he didn't bother much about the grammar. He taught me by crossword puzzles.

STEPHEN (*turning at the fireplace*). Latin crossword puzzles?

LAURA. Yes. He made them up himself.

STEPHEN (*moving below the settee to* C.). What does he do, your father?

LAURA. He's a reporter.

STEPHEN. Here in Rudford?

LAURA. He's on the *Rudford News*. He writes political columns too. He's " Excursus " on the *Kettering Star*, " Audax " on the *Leicester Gazette* and " Scrutator " on the *Buckingham Journal*.

STEPHEN (*leaning on the back of the chair* R. *of the table*). A busy man! You live in the town, don't you?

LAURA. Yes—in Crossdale Avenue.

STEPHEN. Are you a large family?

LAURA. I have a sister; but she's married and lives in New Zealand. There's only my parents and an aunt—she teaches in the Elementary School.

STEPHEN. Are you happy at home?

LAURA. Oh, yes!

STEPHEN (*sitting on the* L. *arm of the settee*). I sometimes wonder about my pupils. They come into my classroom for an hour and sit in the same seats and wear the same clothes—and submit to having their minds improved in a sort of armed neutrality.

LAURA. People are not themselves during school hours.

STEPHEN (*smiling*). I suppose not. Outside, are they different? Have they wit? Animation? Inquiring minds?

LAURA (*with a shy smile*). Animation anyhow.

STEPHEN. Or just excitement at leaving school? Your lot goes out into the big world in—six weeks.

LAURA. Five . . .

STEPHEN. So you're counting the days, eh? Striking them off the calendar?

LAURA. Yes. But not because I want to leave school.

STEPHEN. No? I thought the end of school was the great emancipation? I thought my pupils' marked apathy for the Latin tongue was because their heads were buzzing with the future?

LAURA. I don't like to think of the future. I hate the thought of leaving school.

STEPHEN. That's unusual, surely?

LAURA. I—I . . .

STEPHEN. What?

LAURA. I don't know what I shall do.

STEPHEN. Your career, you mean?

LAURA. No—that's not what I meant. I don't care . . .

STEPHEN. But you must. If you've no plans for the future, perhaps your parents have?

LAURA. They expect me to train as a secretary or something.

STEPHEN. I shouldn't think that was your destiny.

LAURA. I don't know about destiny . . . It's a word my aunt uses a lot.

STEPHEN. In what way? Romantically?

LAURA. Yes.

STEPHEN. Don't let her beguile you. One's character is one's destiny.

LAURA. But if you've nothing to tell you what your character is? I don't know my character—to me it's a muddle.

STEPHEN. That's not unique. But don't let it stay muddled. The mind is free—use its liberty, and be glad of the responsibility. (*He rises and moves up stage.*) Would you like some coffee? I make it myself. I'm the only person in the house who makes good coffee, and all I ask is lots of praise. (*He opens the door, and calls.*) Grace.

GRACE (*off*). Yes?

STEPHEN. The lesson's over. I'm going to make some coffee.

(*He exits, leaving the door open, and goes off* R. GRACE *enters from off* R. *She is an attractive woman, in her early forties, well dressed, but on the arty side. She is educated, but highly-strung; devoted to her husband, and jealous of any outside influence in his life. She gives* LAURA *a brittle smile.*)

GRACE. Well! You've had a long session! I hope it has served some purpose.

LAURA (*rising and standing awkwardly behind her chair*). Oh! Yes . . .

GRACE (*coming down to the chair* L. *of the table*). Shall we get all this out of the way? (*She folds the chair.*) The room doesn't seem itself somehow. (*She takes the chair into the bay window and puts it out of sight below the desk.*)

(LAURA *folds the chair* R. *of the table, and hands it to* GRACE. GRACE *stacks it with the first chair.*)

Thank you.

(LAURA *picks up her satchel and is about to fold the table.*)

(*Stopping* LAURA.) Let me do that. You have to know how it works. It's one of those vicious contraptions. It has a bite like a rat-trap. (*She closes the table with a snap on the last word.*)

LAURA. Shall I put it away for you?

GRACE (*moving up to the door*). No, thank you. I know where it goes.

(*She exits* L. *into the hall, and returns immediately.*)

Would you like to wash your hands? (*She shuts the door.*)

LAURA (*moving to* L. *of the settee*). No, thank you.

GRACE (*coming down stage to the table down* L. *and taking a cigarette*). Well, sit down. Relax.

(LAURA *sits on the settee,* L. *end. She puts the satchel beside her.*)

I've been sitting in my bedroom for nearly two hours listening to the radio.

LAURA. Don't you like the radio?

GRACE (*finding there are no matches, and moving to the desk*). I don't like sitting in my bedroom. To be quite frank, I don't much like school work encroaching on my home life. I hope that doesn't sound unpleasant? (*She lights her cigarette.*)

LAURA. No. I'm sorry.

GRACE. There's nothing to be sorry for. It's just one of those things. When are your examinations? (*She crosses down* R. *to the easy chair.*)

LAURA. They begin on Monday week. They last five days.

GRACE (*sitting*). Whose idea was it that you should have extra coaching in Latin?

LAURA. Mr Barlow's.

GRACE. What do the other pupils say? Doesn't this individual attention suggest favouritism of some kind?

LAURA. Oh, no! He would do the same for anyone.

GRACE (*lightly*). He's never done it before. I hope it doesn't become a habit. I don't know any of my husband's pupils. When I ask him what they're like, he says they're just a row of faces.

(STEPHEN *enters from off* R.)

STEPHEN (*coming down behind the settee*). We'll have to wait a moment for that kettle. Grace, why haven't we got one that whistles ? They're so co-operative.

GRACE. Because I don't want to be a nervous wreck, that's why.

STEPHEN. Laura's father is a journalist. He writes for the *Rudford News*.

GRACE. What's that ? A weekly ?

STEPHEN. Really, darling ! It's the local evening paper.

GRACE. I've never heard of it. What on earth do people find to say in it ?

STEPHEN. In a town of thirty thousand inhabitants all sorts of things go on.

GRACE. Laura, don't you hate Rudford ?

LAURA. Well . . . I was born here. I don't know any other place.

GRACE. How terrible for you. It's the worst kind of provincial town. Oxford ! That's where one should live—or Cambridge. (*She smiles.*) My husband eats his heart out here for lack of conversation. There's no stimulus ; nothing to exercise the mind of an intelligent man.

STEPHEN (*moving up to the door*). It's pretty well exercised earning a living.

(*He exits and goes off* R.)

GRACE (*rising and turning to the mantelpiece*). That dreary High Street on a Saturday morning ! Sometimes this place seems to me to be entirely populated by skittish adolescents from the County School. When we walk through the town I often say to my husband he should wear a false beard.

LAURA (*for something to say*). Because so many people know him ?

GRACE. People ! I'd scarcely call them—people. Those giggly little teenagers with their bold eyes. Most of them look as if they were heading straight for the delinquency courts. This town seems to have a breed of its own. You should know, they're your contemporaries.

LAURA (*uncomfortably*). I don't know any who are—what you say.

GRACE. One glimpse of my husband and their day is made. Isn't it so ?

LAURA (*stammering*). Well—they like him—they respect him.

GRACE. Respect ! They've never heard of it. I'm sorry for them. I'm sorry for their bedraggled little minds, and their nasty little bodies bursting out of their clothes. Don't let's talk about them, it's depressing. Let's talk about something pleasant. Did you notice the garden as you came in ?

LAURA. Yes.

GRACE. It's my great joy. I spend hours working in it while my husband's at school.

LAURA (*after a pause*). Are you lonely in Rudford?

GRACE. Not so lonely as I should be if I became involved in its social life. So I make the life I choose for myself here in my own home, and avoid the comings and goings. To tell you the truth, we are not very sociable. We are inclined to cheat a little so that we can be left alone. Do you like music? (*She sits on the settee,* R. *end.*)

LAURA. Yes, very much.

GRACE. My husband has a wonderful library of records. So we have concerts even though we are a long way from a concert hall—and we are the audience of two. Am I boring you?

LAURA. No. I was just thinking—how lovely it must be to sit and listen quietly. I mean people always talk.

GRACE (*blandly*). Do they? How tiresome! I don't think we do. If we do we don't notice it.

LAURA (*after a pause*). Sometimes they have a concert in the Kimber Hall.

GRACE. We've never been. When the day's work is done we shut our door. Occasionally my husband goes for a walk, that's all. The societies for this and that have given us up, the bridge players have given us up, so we've won the battle for our seclusion. It was quite a fight when we first came here a year ago.

(STEPHEN *enters from off* R. *with a tray of coffee.*)

STEPHEN (*moving behind the settee*). What was a fight? (*He puts the tray on the table.*)

GRACE. Protecting our privacy from the party-givers and whatnots.

STEPHEN (*with a laugh; to* LAURA). My wife is a stay-at-home.

GRACE. Listen to him. One would think I dictated our way of living.

STEPHEN. Well?

GRACE. Darling, we came to the same conclusions early on about living here. We got the hang of the place after we'd been here a couple of months.

STEPHEN. We didn't know it, that's all.

GRACE. You like it now? That's news.

STEPHEN (*pushing down the plunger of the coffee percolator*). Parts of it are lovely. (*He moves down* L. *of the settee.*) Laura, have you ever taken a boat up river towards Ravensbridge?

LAURA. Yes, we often do in the summer. We swim there in the pool.

STEPHEN. I know that pool. The willows touch the water, and the moorhens scurry in and out amongst them.

GRACE. That river smells. All the town sewage goes into it.

STEPHEN (*crossing down* R. *to the easy chair*). If you get on to that line of thought where do you end? On the beach at Cannes I suppose. (*He sits.*)

GRACE. Cannes is different.

STEPHEN. Its sewage isn't.

GRACE. Really, Stephen!

STEPHEN. In the summer we'll go swimming in the pool— Laura shall take us there.

GRACE. Or we could have school picnics, with gay little egg-and-spoon races along the banks. If we are going to take the community to our hearts we really should go the whole hog.

STEPHEN (*embarrassed*). Darling, we're newcomers to this community, and we're not very important to it. Let's shut up about it. (*He rises and crosses up* L. *to the bookshelves. The book he wants is not there. He moves to the desk.*) Laura, at least a third of the Latin papers are bound to centre on Virgil.

(LAURA *rises and moves* L. *of the settee.*)

(*He picks up a small book.*) You ought to read this.

(*They move towards each other.* STEPHEN *hands her the book and their eyes meet.*)

It will give you some idea of his relationship to his own age—the particular moment in history in which he was born.

LAURA. Thank you.

STEPHEN (*crossing behind the settee*). If you can write about him with some authority it might help balance up your weaknesses in other directions. (*He pours out coffee.*)

GRACE. Is it vital to her future that she should be an authority on Virgil's relationship to his age?

STEPHEN. The passing or not-passing of an examination is vital to her immediate future, that's all.

GRACE. How about the others? How do they get on without this special knowledge?

STEPHEN. They'll get by—most of them. Laura, do you take sugar in your coffee?

LAURA. Yes please.

STEPHEN. And milk?

LAURA. No thanks. I like it black.

STEPHEN. There we are. (*He hands her a cup.*)

LAURA. Thank you.

GRACE. This is my husband's one chore. He makes the coffee every evening.

(STEPHEN *hands* GRACE *a cup.*)

And every evening I tell him how excellent it is and how clever he is.

STEPHEN. I've already told her I require lots of praise. (*He moves to* R. *of* LAURA *with his own cup.*)

(LAURA *sips her coffee.*)

LAURA. It's wonderful.
STEPHEN (*laughing, and crossing down* R. *to the easy chair*). Good. I'm glad you like it. (*He sits.*)
GRACE. You're a very shy person, aren't you? Come and sit down. (*She indicates the settee.*)

(LAURA *sits on the settee.*)

I notice a sort of tenseness in the conversation that really isn't necessary. My husband has always told me that the relationship between pupil and teacher is a much more friendly one than in our day. (*With a smile.*) Perhaps it's I who make the conversation difficult?
LAURA (*earnestly*). Oh no! I'm not shy—truly.
STEPHEN (*gently; smiling*). My wife is very direct in her approach—but she means well.
GRACE. Darling, that is what a man says when he apologizes for a fussy mother, or an aunt—she means well.
STEPHEN. I beg your pardon.
GRACE (*appeased and rather coy*). I should say so.
STEPHEN. One is not, after all, madly sure of oneself at seventeen—or very communicative—you've forgotten.
GRACE. You mean it's so long ago?
STEPHEN. Darling, of course I didn't mean that.
GRACE. It is long ago—thank heaven.
STEPHEN. It's Laura's first visit here. She doesn't know us.
GRACE (*lightly, but edged*). She knows you.

(LAURA *is acutely embarrassed.*)

It seems somehow strange that we should be sitting talking about her in the third person as if she weren't here.
STEPHEN (*sharply*). If we are then one of us is being extremely rude. (*He puts his cup on the table, beside the reading lamp.*)
GRACE. Am I? I'm sorry. You must forgive me. But, as I told you, we live in such seclusion here that you probably think I'm very unsociable.
LAURA. No, not at all. I ought to go home. It's getting late.
GRACE. Will you fetch her coat, Stephen. (*She takes* LAURA'S *cup and leans over and puts it, and her own, on the table behind the settee.*)
STEPHEN (*rising*). Yes. Where is it?
GRACE. I left it upstairs in my room.

(STEPHEN *exits and goes off* R. *There is a brief silence.*)

Shall I give you a piece of advice, my dear? You should try to control your imagination.

LAURA. What do you mean?
GRACE (*blandly*). I can sense that you're in love with my husband. I just want you to know that it amuses me—up to a point.

(LAURA *reacts in dismay*.)

(*Kindly*.) I say—up to a point—because I can visualize circumstances in which it might be embarrassing—for him.
LAURA (*in distress*). As if I would ever embarrass him ! (*She rises and moves down* L.)
GRACE. You do admit it?
LAURA (*turning to* GRACE). No ! No !
GRACE. Hush then—forget it.

(STEPHEN *enters with the coat. He looks at* LAURA'S *distressed face, then at* GRACE.)

STEPHEN. What's the matter? (*He comes down* L. *of the settee*.)
GRACE. Nothing. Why must men always say when they come into a silence, "What's the matter?"

(STEPHEN *holds the coat up.* LAURA *moves to him and puts it on, quickly struggling into it as he tries to help. She is pent up and looks as if she would like to rush out of the house*.)

LAURA (*to* GRACE). Good night. (*To* STEPHEN.) Good night, Mr Barlow—and thank you very much.
STEPHEN. Will you be all right, Laura? Shall I walk back with you?
LAURA (*moving up stage*). I'll be all right. (*She goes into the hall*.)

(STEPHEN *follows her into the hall and goes off* L.)

GRACE. You've forgotten your books, my dear. (*She rises, picks up the satchel and moves up stage to the door*.)
LAURA (*taking the satchel*). Thank you.

(*She exits and goes off* L. GRACE *moves down stage below the settee.* STEPHEN *enters, closes the door and crosses to the desk*.)

GRACE. Well that, I should say, is quite a temperamental little piece. (*She sits on the settee,* C.)
STEPHEN (*distantly*). She was shy. You didn't help her much. (*He picks up a pamphlet*.) What devastating information people get hold of. " Three hundred and twenty million people eat with a knife and fork, five hundred and thirty million people use sticks, seven hundred and forty million use their fingers, and one hundred and ninety million use a hunting knife."
GRACE. Who found all that out?
STEPHEN. UNESCO.

GRACE. Why did you bring her here?
STEPHEN. Why should I not have brought her here, dear?
(*He sits at the desk, and opens a book.*)
GRACE. It's been a wasted evening. I listened to the deadliest stuff on the radio.
STEPHEN. There was no reason for you to go and relegate yourself to your bedroom. You could easily have stayed here.
GRACE. There was an atmosphere ... It worried me.
STEPHEN. Atmosphere?
GRACE. Of guilt—frustration—something.
STEPHEN. Whose guilt and whose frustration? (*He looks round at her.*)
GRACE (*after a pause*). There was hostility in the air.
STEPHEN. To whom—from whom?
GRACE. To me—from that girl.
STEPHEN (*turning back to his book*). You're talking nonsense.
GRACE. I'm not talking nonsense. And it's the first time you've charged me with it. Already, you see, there's something. I ask you a question and you reply by another question. You can't expect me to let it slide when the whole perfection of our marriage has been based on our keeping nothing from each other.
STEPHEN. I'm keeping nothing from you that I'm aware of.
GRACE. Except why you asked that girl to the house. The real reason please, Stephen.
STEPHEN. I should have thought it was obvious. (*He turns to her.*) She's below standard in Latin. With a little extra coaching before the exam she might just make it. It was better to bring her here than to keep her in the class-room after hours. That's one of the things you just can't do in a mixed school. (*He turns back to his book.*)
GRACE. Why did we ever come to this wretched town! And that beastly mongrel school that's neither one thing nor the other!
STEPHEN. It's a good school. The educational authorities are very proud of it; it's their show-piece.
GRACE (*after a slight pause*). She's madly in love with you.
(*For a moment* STEPHEN *is silent. He moves slightly in his chair.*)
STEPHEN (*quietly*). Grace dear—be your age.
GRACE (*tensely*). It would have been kinder not to rub that in at the moment.
STEPHEN. "Be your age" is an expression which simply means—be your age. There was nothing sinister in my using it.
GRACE. I could feel her in my bones as she was sitting there. I could hear that adolescent imagination working—seeing herself alone here with you—thinking of herself sleeping in your arms ...

(STEPHEN *puts down his book and rises. He moves to the* L. *end of the settee and stands looking angrily at* GRACE.)

(*In a low tone.*) Sex-mad little tart!
  STEPHEN (*quietly*). What on earth's got into you?
  GRACE (*looking at him*). It's absurd to try to pretend it's news to you that she's in love with you. (*She rises and moves to him.*)
  STEPHEN. Do you suppose I spend my day puzzling out whether or not one of my pupils is in love with me?
  GRACE. There's been something about you lately. You sit behind a book but you're not reading it. You sit in a chair and go off into a trance.

(STEPHEN *crosses to the fireplace and stands with his back to* GRACE.)

  STEPHEN (*with an edge of sarcasm*). It must be my spirit friend taking control.
  GRACE (*moving away* L. *of the settee*). It's her taking control —and you going back on some nostalgic journey to your own youth. (*She turns to him.*) It's you, my dear Stephen, who should remember to be your age.
  STEPHEN (*after a slight pause*). You glean things—like an old woman collecting rubbish—counting it over—muttering to yourself.
  GRACE. Is that how you see me?
  STEPHEN. At the moment—yes. (*He turns to her.*) This kind of conversation could go on all night. It's your sort of game—you're good at it; I'm not. (*He pauses.*) I'll tell you about this girl: she's got what I believe is called a crush on me. I'm quite aware of it. It's been going on for some time. It's upsetting her work, and probably her nerves. One reason I brought her here—apart from the obvious one that she needs coaching—was to meet you—to see us both in our own home. I thought it would be a friendly pleasant evening, and that it might help her to get things in their proper perspective.
  GRACE. It might help *her*! What did you think it would do to me?
  STEPHEN. You're twenty-five years older than she is. I thought you might behave like an intelligent adult.
  GRACE. With her sitting there weighing up what her chances might be against me—counting every line on my face?
  STEPHEN. What lines, Grace?
  GRACE (*moving away* L.; *hysteria creeping in*). Don't be so false! Now I know—I was to be noble. I was to play the role of the self-effacing wife, all detachment and tolerance. Sit back and let your flaming romance crackle on . . .
  STEPHEN. Romance! She's a child. (*He turns to the fireplace and fills his cigarette case from the box on the mantelpiece.*)
  GRACE (*turning to him*). Not such a child—not that one! And well you know it.

(*There is a brief silence.*)

(*She moves towards him, below the settee.*) Don't you?
                (STEPHEN *gives a tired shrug.*)
Anyhow I told her.
    STEPHEN. Told her what?
    GRACE. That I knew she was in love with you.
(STEPHEN *is very quiet. For a moment he is too angry to speak. He turns to* GRACE.)
    STEPHEN. You can't be serious? *Did* you say that?
    GRACE. And I said that it amused me—up to a point. (*She sits on the settee.*)
            (STEPHEN *stares at her incredulously.*)
So it did. She sat there on the sofa like something behind a cage—tame only because there are bars between it and you.
    STEPHEN. You talk like some crazy neurotic—all exaggeration and chatter—silly chatter dressed up to impress yourself. How could you hurt that child? I knew something was going on—I knew by her face when I came in and you made one of your bright covering-up remarks.
    GRACE. All I did was to warn her off. Judging from the way you're carrying on it was high time I did.
    STEPHEN. Have you quite forgotten that age? How vulnerable one is? How serious one is?
    GRACE. You talk as if I were so old that I had forgotten everything.
    STEPHEN. I was talking about her. She is the one who has been hurt—not you.
        (*He moves quickly up to the door and goes off* L.)
    GRACE (*frightened*). Where are you going? (*She rises.*)
    STEPHEN (*off*). Out.
    GRACE (*moving* R. *of the settee and behind it; her voice high-pitched*). You're going to catch up with that little slut . . .
(STEPHEN *appears at the door, angrily wrapping a scarf round his neck.*)
(*Hysterically.*) You subject me to an evening like this till I'm racked with nerves—then you go out and leave me with it all pent up inside me.
    STEPHEN (*looking at her*). You've got rid of quite a lot of it.
    GRACE. Stephen, I'm sorry. I'm sorry. (*She moves up stage to* R. *of the doorway.*) I'm so terrified I'll lose you.
        (STEPHEN *looks at her in a tired preoccupied way.*)
    STEPHEN. How could you lose me? We're tied together by twenty years of life.

GRACE. Is that all?

(*There is a brief pause.*)

Are you going out?
STEPHEN. Yes.
GRACE. Stephen! I have a recurring dream like this. That I am standing at the door—as I am now—begging you not to go out—and you go. And you never come back.
STEPHEN. I shall be back.

(*He goes off* L. *The front door is heard to slam.* GRACE *moves slowly down stage.*)

CURTAIN

SCENE 2

SCENE.—*The same. Two hours later.*

When the CURTAIN *rises, the stage is in darkness except for the reading lamp and a light in the hall.* GRACE *is sitting in the easy chair down* R. *She has an open book on her lap. The door is open. She raises her head and listens.* MRS USHER *crosses the hall from* L. *to* R. *She is the housekeeper, a middle-aged woman dressed in black, with a tatty black bag and an umbrella. As she passes the open door she glances in, sees* GRACE *and stops.*

MRS USHER. I was creeping in quietly, ma'am. I thought you'd have gone to bed.
GRACE. No, not yet. Did you have a nice evening?
MRS USHER (*making a face*). Don't know about nice. I went to my sister's and had an earful as usual. Shall I bolt the front door?
GRACE (*in a stiff little voice*). No. Mr Barlow isn't in yet.
MRS USHER. He's late, isn't he? It's half-past eleven.
GRACE. He went out for a breath of air. It's a lovely night.
MRS USHER. I suppose it is. I never noticed. Well, good night, ma'am.
GRACE. Good night, Mrs Usher.

(MRS USHER *goes, closing the door behind her. The clock chimes the half-hour.* GRACE *looks at it anxiously. She puts her book on the table by the reading lamp and rises. She crosses to the window, parts the curtains and looks out. She wanders restlessly about the room, arrives at the easy chair and sits. Almost at once the front-door bell rings. She rises, runs to the door and exits into the hall off* L.)

HENRY (*off*). Mrs Barlow?
GRACE (*off*). Yes.

HENRY (*off*). I'm Henry Vining—Laura's father. I came to collect her because my wife was getting a little anxious about her coming home alone.

(*There is a slight pause.*)

GRACE (*off*). Won't you come in?
HENRY (*off*). Thank you.

(HENRY *enters from off* L. *He is forty-five; and although he is a small-town journalist he has a scholarly and philosophic personality. He tends to talk—and drink—too much. He moves* R. *of the door.* GRACE *follows him in and leaves the door open.*)

GRACE. She isn't here, Mr Vining. She left about half-past nine. (*She switches on the lights, and moves down* L.C.)

(HENRY *and* GRACE *look at each other, held by the doubts of the moment, but* HENRY *refuses to be alarmed.*)

HENRY. Where on earth can the girl be? It must be getting on for midnight.
GRACE (*glancing at the clock*). It's just after half-past eleven.
HENRY. She must have called in at one of her friends. Thoughtless creatures, children. I don't worry, but her mother does.
GRACE (*stiffly*). Naturally. Do sit down.
HENRY. Thanks. (*He moves to the* R. *end of the settee and slowly takes off his coat.*)
GRACE. Will you have something to drink, Mr Vining?
HENRY. That's a charming idea.

(GRACE *moves up* L. *to the table behind the door.*)

GRACE. A whisky and soda?
HENRY. Wonderful. (*He folds his coat over the arm of the settee.*)

(*There is silence while* GRACE *pours out the drink.*)

I promised my wife faithfully that I wouldn't stop even if I were offered a drink. Where can that girl be?

(GRACE *brings the drink to him below the settee.*)

Thank you.

(GRACE *crosses down* L., *to the table for the cigarettes.*)

The streets are empty and most people seem to be in bed. In this town they draw a line like the equator between night and day. (*He sits on the settee,* R. *end.*)
GRACE (*crossing to* HENRY *with the cigarette box*). It's a grim place—by day or by night. (*She offers him a cigarette.*)
HENRY. You don't like it? Don't smoke, thank you. But

you've an attractive home here and a charming husband, I'm told—though I've never met him.

GRACE (*smiling*). Oh yes, I'm more than content with my home and my husband. I devote my life to them.

HENRY (*casually*). That's as it should be.

GRACE. The typical bourgeois housewife?

HENRY (*smiling*). I don't know what typical means. To me all people are unique. You'd call my wife, I suppose, a bourgeois housewife. But to me, she's the projection of my conscience. (*With a change of tone.*) I'd like to thank your husband for the interest he's taken in my daughter. Is he in?

(GRACE *crosses to the fireplace.*)

GRACE (*after a perceptible pause*). He went out—a few moments ago—for a walk. (*She puts the cigarette box on the mantelpiece, takes a cigarette and turns to him.*) We're on the fringe of the country here, you see. It's very tempting on a night like this. (*She lights her cigarette.*)

HENRY. Quote—" To keep an appointment with a beech tree, or a yellow birch, or an old acquaintance amongst the pines "—unquote. For myself I prefer to look for old acquaintances amongst the wayward flesh. One doesn't have so far to walk. (*He drinks.*) Well, I suppose I ought to go back and make my report on this girl. Perhaps she's home by now.

GRACE. Has she any special friend she might be with? (*She sits in the easy chair.*)

HENRY. No doubt she has. I don't know. Men like me have to keep the most incalculable hours—we know nothing about our families. One day they are little children hanging on your every word and the next they are strange young women who live in your house but are elsewhere in spirit.

GRACE. Shall I ring your home and find out if she's back?

HENRY. Now that requires a little consideration . . . If she's back my poor dear wife will then say where is Henry, what's he doing, send him home at once because the night air affects his chest. For years she has been trying to persuade me the night air affects my chest . . . (*He drinks and glances at* GRACE.)

(GRACE *is silent and preoccupied.*)

Please don't worry about her. She is probably walking hand-in-hand with some young man under the moon.

GRACE (*rising quickly and turning to the fireplace*). Is it usual for her to be out as late as this?

HENRY (*smiling*). No. But the unusual happens. The personality, at that age, seems held together in a very precarious equilibrium—especially hers.

(GRACE *tries not to show too much interest, but there is a certain eagerness in her questioning.*)

GRACE (*turning*). Why especially hers?

(HENRY *sips his drink thoughtfully.*)

HENRY. Because there appears to be a certain revolt against her surroundings . . . (*With a smile.*) She's more intelligent than her mother, and we have a crazy woman who lives with us—my sister, I regret to say. She doesn't help in this period of malaise which some of the young are prone to. (*He finishes his drink.*)

GRACE. You say you know nothing about your daughter . . . I think you know quite a lot.

HENRY (*smiling*). Not until this conversation began. (*He smiles more broadly.*) I'm a reporter, you see. One's half-formed observations need only a little alcohol and a good listener to shape themselves into narrative.

(GRACE *smiles. Unobtrusively she takes his glass and crosses up* L. *to refill it.*)

GRACE. Tell me more about her.

HENRY. What can I tell you? I'm a careless parent. I bob like a cork on the currents and undercurrents of my household. I try to play the role of father but there is no perseverance. One would have to devote time to it—like one of those men with muscles.

(GRACE *returns and hands him his glass.*)

Thank you. (*He smiles.*)

(GRACE *moves away* L.C. HENRY'S *mood is mellow, talkative and amiable. He is unaware of the tenseness in* GRACE'S *questioning.*)

I know her only at second-hand, through my wife who throws me scraps of domestic drama from time to time. She tells me Laura has something on her mind . . . My dear wife thinks human happiness depends on everyone's mind being an amiable blank. (*He drinks.*)

GRACE. What could she have on her mind at her age?

HENRY. Some aspect of sex I suppose. She has the temperament for sharp personal anguish. So had I at her age—I wrote some good poetry.

GRACE (*scarcely able to conceal her perturbation; edgily*). I think you ought to find out what it is—and talk her out of it.

HENRY (*blandly*). I think I know what it is. Her sister was married at seventeen—she had a child when she was eighteen. My little Laura probably thinks life is passing her by. (*He smiles at* GRACE, *but receives no answering smile.*)

GRACE. You treat it very flippantly. (*She points to the clock.*)
Look at the time! And you don't know where she is. (*With
an edge to her voice.*) It's absurd that a girl of her age should
be wandering around loose at this hour, and nobody bothering.
I'm sure Miss Faber would have pretty strong ideas about it
if she knew. (*She crosses to the fireplace and stubs out her cigarette.*)
  HENRY. Who is Miss Faber?
  GRACE. Her headmistress.
  HENRY. Oh! Yes.
  GRACE. As a newspaper man you ought to know the head
of the school your town is so proud of.
  HENRY. I knew her as a woman of immense scholarship—
and a flat chest.
  GRACE (*crossing down* L. *to the telephone; with some asperity*).
Women don't carry their brains in their chest.
  HENRY. Thank heaven. That would really be a serious
anatomical gaff.
  GRACE. I'm going to ring up your wife and find out if she's
back. (*She lifts the receiver.*) What's your number?
  HENRY. Four-one-five.

(GRACE *dials the number.*)

  GRACE (*into the telephone*). Mrs Vining? . . . Mrs Barlow
here . . . Is Laura back yet? . . . Yes, he's here, but not
Laura. She left our house at half-past nine . . . Yes, it must
be . . . Would you like to speak to your husband?

(HENRY *rises and crosses down* L. GRACE *hands him the telephone.
She then crosses to the settee and sits,* L. *end.*)

  HENRY (*into the telephone*). Hello, Vi . . . No dear, I didn't
ring because I thought she'd be home and you'd have gone to
bed . . . Well I'm sure there will be some simple explanation.
She's probably with one of her friends . . . It isn't as late as
all that—it's only a quarter to twelve . . . All right, darling,
don't upset yourself. Give me a moment to collect my thoughts
and decide what to do . . . Yes, I'll come home immediately
. . . Yes, I promise . . . Hush, dear, don't cry . . . I'll be
right home. (*He puts down the receiver.*)

(*There is a moment's worried pause.*)

  GRACE. Your wife doesn't think she's with friends?
  HENRY. No.
  GRACE. If she were somewhere until this hour she would
have telephoned home, wouldn't she?
  HENRY. So her mother says . . . (*He looks at* GRACE.)
How was she when she left here? You asked me a great many
questions about her: (*he moves a little towards* L.C.) she seemed
to have aroused your interest.

GRACE (*unsure of herself; with a little nervous smile*). Did I give that impression? I don't know why. (*With a slight shrug.*) I helped her on with her coat and saw her to the door—and said good night . . .
HENRY. Did she seem depressed in any way about her chances in this examination?
GRACE. I don't know her well enough to say.
HENRY. They worry about such things. They get them out of all proportion.

(*The front door is heard to open and shut.* STEPHEN *appears in the hall, removing his scarf.* GRACE *rises. There is silence in the room as* GRACE *and* HENRY *watch him. He moves out of sight for a moment as he hangs his scarf up. He enters the room and stands just inside the doorway looking at* HENRY.)

GRACE. This is Mr Vining—Laura's father. (*She moves* R. *towards the fireplace.*)
HENRY. Good evening.
STEPHEN. How do you do? (*He closes the door.*)
GRACE (*in a high tense voice*). Laura isn't home yet.

(STEPHEN *looks at* GRACE, *then to* HENRY. *There is consternation on his face, and for a moment he does not speak.*)

HENRY. My wife sent me to fetch her. We've just telephoned home—she isn't there.

(STEPHEN *is deeply perturbed. He frowns nervously and glances at his wrist-watch.*)

STEPHEN. But she—she must be. (*He comes down to the* L. *end of the settee.*)
HENRY. I assure you . . . I've just spoken to my wife; she's already in tears.
GRACE (*her voice taut and strained; to* STEPHEN). You didn't see her when you were out?
STEPHEN (*after a slight pause; without looking at her*). No.
GRACE. Is she so elusive? Too bad.
STEPHEN. Grace! Please!
HENRY (*quietly*). Is there something you know that I don't?

(GRACE *stares at* STEPHEN.)

GRACE (*after a tense pause*). She is in love with my husband.

(HENRY *takes this in. He looks gravely and incredulously at* STEPHEN.)

HENRY (*very quietly; to* GRACE). You can't be taking this seriously—she's a child.
GRACE (*bitterly*). Is she?

Sc. 3]   THE DAY'S MISCHIEF   19

STEPHEN. Grace, will you leave us? I want to talk to Mr Vining.

GRACE. Why should I leave you? What have you got to say to him that I can't hear?

HENRY (*to* GRACE). Please leave us together for a moment, Mrs Barlow. I am suddenly very anxious about my daughter; (*he moves to* STEPHEN) I want to know whatever there is to know.

GRACE (*wildly*). I won't go! Your anxiety is nothing to mine. I've got more at stake.

HENRY (*turning quickly to* STEPHEN). When you were out just now, Mr Barlow—were you with my daughter?

STEPHEN. Yes.

(GRACE *turns to the fireplace. She bites her lip to control her emotion. She is on the edge of hysteria.*)

HENRY (*presently; very controlled*). This is a little disturbing. At any rate there's no mystery as to her whereabouts. You've just taken her home, have you?

STEPHEN. No I haven't. I put her on a bus at the bridge at about half-past ten—at least I watched from the path. I saw the bus stop and go on again. I thought it was unwise for both of us that we should be seen together at that hour.

HENRY. If she had been on the bus she would have been home in ten minutes—less.

STEPHEN. Yes.

HENRY (*bursting out*). Then where is she, for God's sake?

STEPHEN (*softly*). I don't know.

(GRACE *turns quickly and looks at* STEPHEN *in anguish.*)

QUICK CURTAIN

SCENE 3

SCENE.—*The living-room of the* VININGS' *house. Three days later. Evening.*

The room is a place to live in, and HENRY *and* VI *are not décor conscious. The furniture was bought when they were married and neither has any reason for changing it. At the back a glass door leads to the garden.* R. *of this another door leads into the hall. The fireplace is in the* L. *wall, and has a club fender; near it is the settee. A small table down* R. *is shared by the telephone and the whisky. A recess in the* R. *wall houses the dining table and sideboard. Down stage,* R.C., *there is a gate-legged table with two chairs. An easy chair below the fireplace, and a small table or desk near the garden door, above which hangs a draped bird-cage, completes the furniture.*

(*See the Ground Plan at the end of the Play.*)

When the CURTAIN *rises,* EVELYN VINING *is standing above the table* R.C. *looking through the contents of a drawer. She is* HENRY'S *sister; a frustrated and rather strange spinster of forty who has built her life on a love-affair of her youth.* VI *enters from the hall. She is* HENRY'S *long-suffering and devoted wife. She is in her late thirties, and is several degrees below her husband in mentality. She looks at the bird-cage.*

VI (*moving slowly down* C. *to the settee*). Who covered Peter up?

EVELYN (*taking some photographs out of a packet*). I did. He was singing. (*She looks through the photographs.*)

VI (*moving up stage to the bird-cage*). Where's Henry gone? (*She takes off the cover, and moves down* L. *of the settee.*)

EVELYN. He went back to the police station. One of the search parties has just come in.

VI (*sitting on the settee,* R. *end*). He must be worn out.

EVELYN. He had about an hour's sleep in the chair. Vi dear, what are you wandering about for? Three days now you've done nothing but wander about in that old dressing-gown.

VI. What else can I do?

EVELYN. You could dress, dear. Or you could stay in bed. What do you think you've had all those sleeping pills for? (*She puts the photographs back in the packet and the packet in the drawer.*)

VI. They don't do anything except slow everything up. I can't speak properly. I feel as weak as a cat.

EVELYN. They've found something, Vi.

VI. What?

EVELYN. Her beret. (*She pulls a pink leaflet from the drawer and looks at it.*)

VI. Are they sure it's hers?

EVELYN. It has her name in it.

VI. Where did they find it?

EVELYN. In a bush somewhere below the bridge.

VI (*breaking down*). Oh . . .

(EVELYN *drops the leaflet in the drawer, crosses silently to* VI *and slips a cushion behind her head, then she returns to the table and continues her sorting. The two women are silent with their unspoken thoughts between them.*)

(*Presently.*) I was remembering things about her . . . Do you remember when she thought the equator was an imaginary lion running round the earth?

EVELYN (*stolidly*). So it is. (*She sits* R. *of the table and opens a packet of old letters.*)

VI. No, a lion—l-i-o-n. She thought it kept on running and running round the earth.

EVELYN (*without a smile*). That's just plain silly.

VI (*looking at her with childish resentment*). It isn't silly. She was only six. The trouble about trying to talk to you is you've no sense of humour.

EVELYN (*reading a letter*). I don't see how anyone can have a sense of humour at this time.

VI (*crying weakly*). I'm her mother and I would give my life's blood for her . . . Why doesn't Henry come back ? (*She rises and moves to the fireplace.*)

EVELYN (*kindly but firmly*). These drugs are making you childish. You'd better try and get a grip on yourself.

(VI *turns and stares resentfully at* EVELYN.)

VI. Is that drawer hers ?
EVELYN. Yes.
VI. You've no business to touch her things.
EVELYN. Henry asked me to. (*Patiently.*) I'm never one to pry, you know that, Vi. Henry wanted to spare you having to do it.

VI (*crossing slowly to* L. *of the table* R.C.). What are you looking for ?

EVELYN. Anything that would give us a clue to what might have been going on in her life. They're stuck, you see. They don't know where to turn.

VI. I knew everything that was going on in her life.
EVELYN. Nobody knows everything about another person. (*She returns a letter to its envelope and does up the packet.*)
VI. She had no secrets from me.
EVELYN. Everybody has secrets.
VI. You think everybody's like yourself.
EVELYN (*patiently*). Not at all. I'm unusual. And I know it.
VI. Because of that damned ghost you live with.
EVELYN (*tolerantly*). Don't let us talk about him, please.
VI. I don't want to talk about him, I'm sure. (*She turns up towards the hall door.*) I'm sick to death of him.

(EVELYN *gives a resigned shrug. She finds the pink leaflet in the drawer and examines it.*)

EVELYN. What do you think this would mean ? *Bate's Cure for Blushing.*

VI (*turning and coming down* C.). I wish you'd leave her things alone.

EVELYN. That would point to her knowledge of her own self-consciousness and a desire to overcome it.

VI. What would you know about it ? (*She moves below the settee to the fireplace.*) You've never blushed in your life. (*She sits on the fender.*)

EVELYN. Vi dear, you're not yourself. You're saying things under the influence of those barbiturates that you would never

say normally. We're friends, Vi. We've always been good friends, haven't we, dear?
Vi. No.
Evelyn (*indulgently*). You know we have. But you can pick on me as much as you like—I know you're in great trouble. I don't take umbrage. (*She finds a tattered paper-covered book, and looks at it.*) This looks like a book she shouldn't have had. It was hidden under the paper. (*She rises.*)
Vi. Did you never hide a book under the paper of a drawer?
Evelyn. *Black Spring.* (*She opens it at random.*)
Vi. Give it to me.

(Evelyn *crosses slowly below the settee.*)

Evelyn. It looks like a banned book.
Vi. Every girl gets hold of a banned book at some time or other. They go round the schools. Girls read them out of curiosity.
Evelyn. Did you know she had it? (*She turns over a few pages.*)
Vi. No.
Evelyn. So you see you don't know *every*thing about her, Vi.
Vi (*rising*). Give it to me. And don't tell Henry.

(Evelyn *hands her the book and crosses back to the table* R.C. *and sits.*)

(*She puts the book behind a cushion on the settee without even glancing at it.*) I told her all there was to know about sex years ago. She wasn't even interested. (*She sits on the settee.*)
Evelyn (*taking a cigarette from a packet on the table*). Pardon me if I smile.
Vi. What is there to smile at?
Evelyn. The idea of you telling her *all* there was to know about sex. (*She lights her cigarette.*)
Vi. Well?
Evelyn. Sex has innumerable aspects. It's a very complex subject.
Vi. Not to me it isn't. Which of us should know? I've been married twenty years and I've had two children.
Evelyn (*untying a bundle of letters*). That's nothing, my dear Vi. You're still as innocent as a child.
Vi (*rather peevishly*). I don't like this patronizing. I've known it, and I've grown out of it in the proper way. You're morbid about it because you've never known it.
Evelyn (*after a moment's silence; drily*). It looks as if Laura's interest was also morbid—as you call it.
Vi. There's nothing like that about her except what she gets off you. There was never anything queer in my family—it's you it comes from.

EVELYN. I told you you weren't yourself. (*She ties up the letters.*) I know I have a life of my own which may seem peculiar to you. But to me it is perfectly normal.

VI. Going to bed with a ghost every night!

EVELYN. In my sleep I live my own life. I've never made any secret of it. It's got nothing to do with our present trouble and there's no need to bring it up. I don't see why you should suddenly turn vindictive towards me, Vi. It isn't like you, dear. You've always been sympathetic and understanding. (*She opens a small purse.*)

VI. I'm sick of it. Laura was probably sick of it too. That's why she's run away.

EVELYN (*rather sharply*). Is that what you're thinking?

VI. It's what Henry thinks too. Living with you addles people's brains. You coming down all mysterious in the morning as if you'd spent the night in a brothel.

(EVELYN *draws in her breath sharply. She closes the purse and replaces it. She opens a calendar.*)

EVELYN (*trying to be patient*). You haven't the faintest idea of what goes on in a brothel, Vi. You're a nice woman trying to be nasty for some reason unknown to me. You've decided to be spiteful because you're so tired out you don't know what to do with yourself.

VI. What sort of atmosphere was it for a young girl to be brought up in? You lose the first man you fall in love with, but that was a long time ago. So you make an idol out of him and live an indecent life with him in your dreams.

EVELYN (*stung at last*). Indecent? You have no experience of a first love that turns to tragedy. (*She replaces the calendar.*)

VI. I would have set out to forget it. I would have looked for someone else.

EVELYN (*picking out a jar of ointment*). That makes me shudder. (*She sniffs at the jar.*)

VI. You've never even tried to make friends except with other women.

EVELYN (*fiercely*). What's that got to do with it?

VI. You might have met some other man and been happier.

EVELYN (*rising*). You don't know what you're talking about. (*She moves above the table and stubs out her cigarette in the ashtray on the* L. *side of the table.*)

VI. You've got everybody in this house obsessed with it, Henry says. He can't sleep lately for the thought of you and your dreams in the next room. How do you know Laura didn't feel the same?

EVELYN (*drily*). It's taken a long time for Henry to feel that way about it. (*She picks out a wallet and examines it.*)

Vi. Only since he was afraid for Laura. He doesn't think it funny any more.

Evelyn. Who said it was ever funny? (*She puts down the wallet and picks up a small duster.*)

Vi. Henry and I. We used to think it was funny—but not any more.

Evelyn. I have a happy life. I'm happy in my own way and I am secure in my happiness. It doesn't matter to me what people think. Nobody can ever take my sure and certain happiness away from me; and that's more than most people can say. More than you can say, Vi—you think you're happy with Henry. (*She replaces all the contents of the drawer.*)

Vi. I *am* happy with Henry.

Evelyn. Your love is complacent—a matter of habit. He's forgotten what love is. He drinks. He stays out late. You quarrel.

Vi. That's part and parcel of marriage. Our quarrels don't mean a thing. I love Henry dearly and he loves me. I'd rather have Henry beside me whatever he was like than have your kind of carrying on with a disembodied spirit.

Evelyn. You misunderstand. (*She looks at some empty talcum powder boxes in the drawer.*) All I have ever tried to say is that love does not need the physical presence. I know absolute love, and I am happy and fortunate beyond all other women.

Vi (*rising; wearily*). Nuts. Just nuts. That's all I can say to you. (*She staggers slightly.*)

Evelyn (*crossing to* Vi). You see, it's these drugs. You'd never have said any of this if you'd been yourself. Come and lie down on your bed again, there's a good girl.

(*She leads* Vi *up to the hall door and they exit. There is a moment's pause, then* Henry *enters from the garden, from off* L. *He is very weary. He crosses down* R. *to the table and pours himself a large whisky. He looks round for the water, sees it on the sideboard and moves up to collect it. He comes down* R. *pouring water into the glass.* Evelyn *enters from the hall.*)

Henry, those Latin text-books she would have taken to the Barlows that night—I found them down the side of her bed. I didn't tell Vi. (*She comes down to the* R. *end of the settee.*)

Henry (*moving to the table* R.C.). I don't see what that means. (*He sits* R. *of the table.*)

Evelyn. She must have come in and gone out again, while Vi and I were at the pictures. We got back here about ten.

Henry (*frowning and puzzled*). I don't see that it makes any difference . . . Why would they be down the side of her bed?

Evelyn. She must have come in and lain down on her bed and the books slipped down the side.

HENRY (*wearily*). Yes. It doesn't seem to add anything to what we know : she came in and went out and met someone . . . How is Vi ?

EVELYN. She hasn't slept. I don't think those pills suit her. They confuse her without sending her to sleep. I think you ought to let the police know that Laura came in.

HENRY (*wearily*). Yes. I'll tell them. (*He pauses. Without looking at* EVELYN.) They've started dragging operations on the river.

(EVELYN *stares at* HENRY, *turns and moves below the settee and rearranges the cushions.*)

EVELYN. Have they any reason to think they'll find her there ?

HENRY. They seem to have come to some conclusion . . . (*Bitterly.*) Where can she be ? She's vanished off the face of the earth.

EVELYN (*after a pause*). Henry—are you blaming yourself for this ? (*She sits on the settee.*)

HENRY (*absently*). Blame ? Blame will come later, and will be futile anyhow. (*He rises, moves* R. *to the table and pours himself another drink.*)

EVELYN (*timidly*). Do you think you ought to drink when you're so tired ?

HENRY. I don't think, my dear Evelyn—I know. My mind is full of horrors. Whichever way it turns it runs into horror.

EVELYN (*rising and moving above the table* R.C.). I looked through her things.

HENRY. Yes ?

EVELYN. I didn't find anything of importance. Letters, odds and ends ; a booklet called *Bate's Cure for Blushing* . . .

HENRY (*shaking his head slowly in compassion ; murmuring*). Poor child.

EVELYN (*picking up the drawer*). There was a calendar with some odd marks on it.

HENRY (*with slight dubious interest*). A calendar ?

EVELYN. I couldn't make anything of it. (*She is about to move* L. *with the drawer.*)

HENRY. Give it to me, will you.

(EVELYN *puts the drawer down on the table and rummages in it until she finds the calendar. She hands it to* HENRY. HENRY *looks at it intently.* EVELYN *takes the drawer up* L. *and puts it on the table near the garden door.*)

(*To himself.*) Time. She has been so concerned with the passing of time. (*He puts the calendar in his pocket and looks at* EVELYN.) Has Vi said anything to you about Laura and Barlow ? (*He sits* R. *of the table.*)

EVELYN (*coming down to the back of the settee*). No—but I know.

HENRY (*bitterly*). It appears that he was her Great Love.

(EVELYN *is astounded. Then a slow ruminative smile passes across her face.*)

EVELYN. Yes. It's strange . . . Very strange, Henry.

HENRY (*irritated by her tone and expression*). It isn't as strange as that. It's understandable enough.

EVELYN. But he was the first and he was unattainable. I always knew that Laura was me. Her destiny, you see, was running on parallel lines to mine.

HENRY. Evelyn, don't let's have any destiny nonsense. I never could stand it and I can stand it less at the moment. Laura was nothing like you. You've always been—let's face it —a shade eccentric.

EVELYN. Only to you and Vi with your unimaginative married life.

HENRY (*crisply*). Our married life suits us both very well, thank you.

EVELYN. But love, Henry—you've forgotten all about love, haven't you?

HENRY. I'm not a victim of it—by vocation—as you are. It's there—assimilated into my middle-aged life and it gives me no trouble. What more would one ask?

EVELYN. Love is of the spirit—it has nothing to do with your commonplace substitute, Henry. Perhaps that's what Laura ran away from.

(HENRY *shoots an angry glance at* EVELYN.)

HENRY (*controlling himself*). Love at our age, old girl, is kindness. That could never give offence to the young. Perhaps it was you she ran away from.

EVELYN (*with an indulgent shrug*). Poor Henry! The years have made you so blind—you clutch at a whisky glass to clear your vision.

(*The front-door bell rings.*)

There's someone at the door.

(*She exits to the hall.*)

HENRY (*calling after her*). I clutch it to keep my temper, you crazy girl.

STEPHEN (*off*). Could I have a word with Mr Vining?

EVELYN (*off*). Are you Mr Barlow? Would you go down the passage, please—first on the right.

(STEPHEN *enters from the hall. He carries his hat.* EVELYN *follows him in and shuts the door.*)

STEPHEN. I don't expect a welcome, but I wanted to see you. (*He comes down below the settee.*)
HENRY (*withdrawn*). I hear you've been out with the search parties all the week-end. I haven't got round to thanking people yet.
STEPHEN. No-one is looking for thanks. They've indicated that they prefer me to keep out of it anyhow.
HENRY. Sit down, won't you.

(STEPHEN *sits on the settee. He puts his hat down beside him.* EVELYN *comes down to the chair above the table* R.C. *and sits.*)

Evelyn ; go and see if Vi is all right. Keep her in her room.

(EVELYN *gives* HENRY *a look, rises and exits to the hall.*)

I've told my wife as little as possible of what is going on outside.
STEPHEN. It's as well. How is she?
HENRY (*briefly*). Living on sedatives. Wandering around in a sort of twilight sleep. She'd be out of her mind otherwise. Will you have a drink? (*He rises and moves* R. *to the table.*)
STEPHEN. No, thanks.
HENRY. You know, I suppose, that the whole town has got its finger pointed at you? (*He pours himself a drink.*)
STEPHEN (*quietly*). I can scarcely help knowing.

(*There is a brief silence.*)

HENRY. I have a hatred of injustice. I try to remain unbiased until the truth is revealed—but it is not easy. (*He moves up stage and sits against the edge of the dining table.*)
STEPHEN. I'm grateful to you for that much. I've had an humiliating afternoon. The pupils went on strike : they refused to attend my classes ; I was hissed in the corridors. Later Miss Faber suggested that I send in my resignation—which I've done.

(HENRY *drinks slowly and thoughtfully in silence.*)

HENRY. The pupils have been very active with their theories.
STEPHEN. That was to be expected.
HENRY. There's been some wild talk.
STEPHEN (*bitterly*). Wild exaggerations.
HENRY. Who is to say? They knew her better than I did. The police have been building up a picture of her life —I don't recognize it. A lonely girl given to days of silence and long walks alone by the riverside. The headmistress has been examining her work—essays, comments, opinions. They're subtle and mature. To me she was a child.
STEPHEN. She wasn't a child. None of them are children.

(*There is a pause.* HENRY *comes down to the chair* R. *of the table* R.C. *and sits.*)

HENRY. The police have started dragging the river.
STEPHEN. I know. I've just come from the police station.
HENRY. What am I to do with my wife if they find her there ? What do we become ? Old sad people staring into the fire wondering where we failed. (*He suddenly looks piercingly at* STEPHEN.) Do *you* think they'll find her there ?
STEPHEN. I don't know any more than you do.
HENRY (*quietly*). That is a lie.
STEPHEN. As you like.

(HENRY *takes a sip of his drink, rises and crosses to the fireplace.*)

HENRY. I'm sorry. That was a dramatic statement made only because the opening occurred. I catch myself doing it these days and feel rather ashamed afterwards.

(STEPHEN *looks at him with a slight surprised smile.*)

I once covered a story something like this. I find myself checking up on how much I missed. The father gives way to the journalist—an ignominious creature who sees himself as the burning centre with events spinning round him. (*He drinks.*) When drama hits people who are not used to it there is a falseness of reaction which is very disturbing. An element of play-acting creeps in in spite of oneself.
STEPHEN. In your position perhaps. Not in mine. I am isolated, with a tide of hate rising against me.

(*There is a brief silence.*)

HENRY. On what grounds exactly were you asked to resign ?
STEPHEN. There was a detail which I hadn't mentioned before because I thought Laura would come back and that it wouldn't be necessary. Today I told Miss Faber and also the police.
HENRY. What was the detail ?
STEPHEN. That I *asked* Laura to meet me. She was already home—I telephoned her. The fact that I made an assignation with a pupil commits me to—dismissal.

(HENRY *crosses to* L. *of the table* R.C.)

HENRY. Where did you ask her to meet you ?
STEPHEN. On the Castle Hill road—below the bridge.
HENRY. Why ?
STEPHEN. She was on my conscience. She had been hurt, I thought. I thought that if I talked to her I could make amends in some way.
HENRY. You said you met her by accident.
STEPHEN. Well, that was the easy way out. I didn't foresee that things would become as serious as this.

(*There is a pause.*)

HENRY. Were you in love with my daughter?
STEPHEN (*after a moment's hesitation*). I had never admitted it to myself until that night. If I loved her, it was from a distance —from a long way off. In the way the dead might love the living.
HENRY. So you tell yourself now. As you begin to feel the weight of public opinion, you take the trouble to come here to persuade me that your interest in my daughter was something remote and benevolent.

(STEPHEN *gives a slight weary shrug.*)

(*He moves round to* R. *of the table* R.C. *Bursting out.*) How do I know that it was? The police have got their eyes hard on you. Maybe the fight to preserve your own life has already begun in you.
STEPHEN (*quietly*). I *may* have to fight for my life. I can see that on its way.
HENRY (*turning and moving* L. *of the table*). So you come to me! What for? To get *me* on your side? You were in love with my daughter whatever label you put on it. What happens to that kind of love? You crush and repress it because of your marriage until it corrupts itself; then suddenly puts forth some monstrous flower. (*He turns away.*)
STEPHEN (*quietly*). I have never harmed her. That is what I came to tell you.
HENRY (*raising his voice*). Then where is she, man? Is she dead or alive? (*He turns to* STEPHEN.)
STEPHEN (*wearily*). I can't answer that any more than you can.

(HENRY *moves down* R. *to the table and pours himself another drink.*)

HENRY (*in a normal voice*). I scarcely know you, Barlow. When you tell me you have never harmed my daughter I want to believe you. You've all the outward signs of the civilized mind, but I've been a newspaper man too long to be beguiled by that. We often meet them—the doctors, scoutmasters, ministers of religion, who suddenly find a frightening spotlight on themselves. I've been ashamed to ask them the questions I had to. I've turned aside from the sight of them forced to carry their private lives in public, like sandwich-men.
STEPHEN (*bitterly*). I'm beginning to get a taste of that.
HENRY. You're beginning to get a picture of where you stand. Alone in a draughty station where the trains have stopped running. So you come to me. Why to me of all people? (*Harshly.*) I'm now facing only two possibilities about my daughter—suicide—or some crime against her. (*He sits* R. *of the table* R.C.)

STEPHEN. I guessed you would be down to that. That's chiefly why I came to see you—to save you, if I could, from torturing yourself; to assure you I am a perfectly normal man and quite incapable, as far as I know, of physical violence of any kind.

HENRY (*morosely*). They all talk like that. When the passion of a thing is over they are clear—lucid—more normal than the normal. They are polite and restrained too, like you.

(STEPHEN *rises. He picks up his hat.*)

STEPHEN. There's nothing more to say then, is there?

HENRY. Couldn't you have seen—if you had been the normal person you say you are—that any relationship between a master and his pupil had the very texture of catastrophe in it?

STEPHEN. There was no relationship.

HENRY. A situation then.

STEPHEN. Not until that night.

HENRY (*after a pause*). The more I talk to you the more ominous the thing becomes.

STEPHEN (*obviously on edge; moving to* L. *of the table* R.C.; *urgently*). Mr Vining—please believe me. I am not a seducer.

HENRY. Why then telephone a girl of seventeen to meet you late at night in an isolated spot?

STEPHEN. It had to be an isolated spot. You know this town. I couldn't be seen with her—or she with me. And I had to talk to her. At least I thought I had to.

HENRY. To teach her the first steps in shaping her love for you—to your conventional environment.

STEPHEN. To teach her nothing.

HENRY. To make love to her then. Why else?

(STEPHEN *is silent.*)

(*Very quietly.*) Now let us have the truth.

STEPHEN. The truth is complicated. (*He breaks away* L. *to the fireplace.*)

HENRY. Uncomplicate it.

STEPHEN. One would have to differentiate between the planes and degrees of love.

HENRY (*raising his voice*). To hell with the degrees of love!

(STEPHEN *is silent.* HENRY *glares at him.*)

You are about to tell me that you loved her as a brother—or as a father.

STEPHEN. Will you listen to me if I try to—find—the truth?

(HENRY *rises, moves* R. *to the table and refills his glass.*)

(*He moves below the settee.*) I have been aware of her for some time. There was a new excitement in my daily life—the excitement of her face, her presence. Sometimes, as she sat opposite me in class, I was back in the days of my own innocence, having forgotten all I had learned in between. (*He moves up stage* R. *of the settee.*) Afterwards I would take myself to task, I would ask myself what I thought I was up to. There was no answer to that. There existed between us a state of love—suspended in the air, (*he moves behind the settee*) with no past, no future, and no present. That is how it was.

(HENRY *moves up stage and sits against the edge of the dining table. He sips his drink and listens impassively.*)

I have tried to analyse what made me ask her to my house. Curiosity perhaps—or a sense of urgency because soon she would be leaving school and going out of my world—or perhaps just a desire to know her better. (*He moves to the chair above the table* R.C.) When my wife questioned me about that I was not particularly truthful. (*He sits.*)

HENRY. Your wife was jealous of her?
STEPHEN. We quarrelled after Laura left.
HENRY. *About* Laura?
STEPHEN. Yes. My wife is a very direct person; she brought things out into the open and told Laura that she knew. Laura went home. Shortly after that I went out. I wanted to see her. In the mood of the moment I telephoned her. I felt there had been some unnecessary hurt—some cruelty which I should try to put right.
HENRY. You were very much in love with her at that point?
STEPHEN. I felt a great tenderness towards her—a responsibility for her.
HENRY. And a great desire to make love to her.
STEPHEN (*after a pause*). Yes.
HENRY (*bitterly*). So we come to the seduction scene.
STEPHEN. We don't.

(HENRY *looks at* STEPHEN. *He rises and comes down stage* R. *of the table* R.C.)

HENRY. When I called at your house that night to collect Laura your wife told me you had been out only for a few minutes, when you had in fact been out for over two hours. Why did she say that?
STEPHEN. I've no idea.
HENRY. Short of some pre-knowledge that all this was going to happen it was very quick action on her part—covering up for you. Perhaps she had reason to fear for your reputation?
STEPHEN. Never until now. My wife and I . . . We have been for years very much attached to one another. Everything has been right with our marriage.
HENRY. Yet you fell in love with my daughter?

STEPHEN. Yes.

(HENRY *meditates for a moment.*)

HENRY (*grudgingly*). What you say has the ring of truth.

STEPHEN (*quietly*). It's generous of you to say so—in this fog of suspicion. (*He rises.*)

HENRY. What state of mind was she in when you left her?

STEPHEN (*slowly*). Quiet. A little tense, as indeed I was too. The whole incident had been a hail and farewell. I saw her on to the bus—as I thought. Then I went back and walked over the Castle Hill.

HENRY. And she—where did she go? Where in God's name did she go? The river? If all is as you say, I can't believe that. (*He broods for a moment, then looks at* STEPHEN.) Can you?

STEPHEN. I don't know any more.

HENRY (*heavily*). Well—we shall soon know. (*He puts his glass on the table.*) Will you have a drink?

STEPHEN. No, thanks. I must go home. (*He moves slowly to the hall door.*)

HENRY. You've paid pretty dearly for this—this idyll. Your job—your career . . .

STEPHEN. There will be time enough to think about that . . .

HENRY. I'm sorry. Forgive my harshness, won't you. It's this horrible hiatus we live in. We lose sight of our habits. (*He moves up stage to* STEPHEN.)

STEPHEN. I feel easier in my mind for having talked to you. I knew you would be beset by all kinds of fears. Good-bye.

HENRY. Good-bye.

(STEPHEN *exits to the hall.* HENRY *closes the door. He crosses below the settee to look at the clock on the mantelpiece.* EVELYN *enters from the hall.*)

EVELYN (*shutting the door*). What did he have to say? (*She comes down to the table* R.C.)

HENRY (*sitting moodily on the settee*). Nothing much. He's going through hell. Hell on earth must be the combination of certain sets of circumstances. He's right in the middle of them.

EVELYN (*sitting on the chair above the table*). I wish you hadn't sent me out of the room. I could have helped. I was thinking upstairs that all my knowledge has been accumulating just to meet this crisis.

HENRY (*drily*). Let's hope it won't be needed.

EVELYN. It will be—and I think I know who will need it.

HENRY. So long as it isn't me . . . (*He looks shrewdly at* EVELYN.) Don't you go poking your nose into this.

(*The front-door bell rings.*)

Sc. 3] THE DAY'S MISCHIEF 33

(*He rises. Quickly.*) I'm not in. I don't want to see anyone.
(*He moves to the fireplace and stands with his back to it.*)

(EVELYN *rises and exits to the hall. She leaves the door open.*)

SALLY (*off*). Good evening, Miss Vining. We've called to see Laura's mother, if we can. There's something we want to talk to her about.

EVELYN (*off*). Well—she's resting at the moment. If you'll just wait there I'll see if Mr Vining will see you.

(*She enters and comes down to the* R. *end of the settee.*)

It's Sally, Laura's friend, and another girl. They want to see Vi.

HENRY. They can't see Vi.

EVELYN. They're a sort of deputation. I think you ought to hear what they have to say.

HENRY (*wearily*). All right.

(EVELYN *moves up to the hall door and calls.*)

EVELYN. All right, Sally, Mr Vining will see you.

(SALLY *and* PHOEBE *enter from the hall. They are school friends of* LAURA'S; *aged sixteen or seventeen. Both are self-conscious. They are grave and impressed by the occasion.*)

SALLY (*coming down* L. *of the table* R.C.). Good evening, Mr Vining. This is Phoebe. She's a friend of Laura's too.

(HENRY *smiles.* EVELYN *shuts the door; then comes down stage and sits* R. *of the table* R.C.)

PHOEBE (*crossing to* HENRY; *politely*). I hope we're not intruding.

HENRY. Not at all. We're shut in here with nothing to do. Sit down, won't you.

PHOEBE. It was really Laura's mother we were supposed to see. (*She sits on the settee,* R. *end.*)

HENRY. She's asleep, I'm afraid. She's going through a bad time.

SALLY (*moving to the chair above the table and sitting*). We all feel terrible about it, Mr Vining—all the girls. Nobody can think about anything else. But we knew . . . (*She stops suddenly and looks at* PHOEBE.) Phoebe had better tell you.

PHOEBE. Well, the class thought I should be spokeswoman . . .

(HENRY *looks at her; waiting.*)

SALLY (*impulsively*). You'll be very angry. And we're not saying anything against Laura. I was her best friend. I mean I am.

PHOEBE. We just want to see that the person responsible gets his deserts.

HENRY (*politely*). Responsible for what?

(SALLY *looks at* PHOEBE.)

PHOEBE. For whatever has happened to her . . . We don't like telling you but we had a meeting after school and the girls all thought it was our duty . . . It's about Mr Barlow . . .

HENRY. Yes?

SALLY. Mr Vining—in the last few months Laura became quite different to what she used to be.

HENRY (*detached*). In what way?

SALLY. She wasn't one of us any more. Just different; wasn't she, Phoebe?

PHOEBE. It was Mr Barlow. She had a terrible crush on him and he used to lead her on. In class he never took his eyes off her.

HENRY. You're sure you're not exaggerating things?

EVELYN. Henry, let them say what they have to say.

SALLY. We wouldn't exaggerate, Mr Vining. Because we don't want to—to add to your troubles. But it's dreadfully serious. Tell him, Phoebe. (*She rises and moves to the* R. *end of the settee.*) Begin at the beginning.

PHOEBE. Well, she used to go for walks alone along by the river and up the Castle Hill road.

HENRY. So I believe.

PHOEBE. Well, so did Mr Barlow.

(*There is a slight pause.*)

SALLY. Mr Vining, I hope you won't think we're trying to blacken Laura's name or anything, will you? Because I would be the last . . .

HENRY (*to* PHOEBE). What else?

PHOEBE. It's been going on for months. He would go along the road alone and then shortly afterwards Laura would follow. Doris Morgan's mother has seen them often—the Morgans who live in that white house by the bridge.

HENRY (*tenser*). Has she seen them together?

PHOEBE. No, that's the point. They wouldn't want to be seen together—at least he wouldn't. He's got a wife and they say she watches him like a cat. (*She turns to* SALLY.) You tell him what Laura said to you.

(SALLY *swallows and crosses to* HENRY.)

SALLY. She said to me one night—you know the funny way she used to talk sometimes like out of a book—she said she was living in the shadow of an hour-glass.

EVELYN. Obsessed with the passing of time. You said it yourself, Henry.

PHOEBE (*like a witness*). All the evidence we collected led to the same conclusion.
HENRY (*puzzled but tense*). What conclusion? (*He sits in the easy chair down* L.)
(SALLY *and* PHOEBE *look at each other, each waiting for the other to say it.*)
(*Quietly.*) Tell me.
SALLY (*to* PHOEBE). Tell him.
PHOEBE. That she was pregnant—or she was afraid she was.

(HENRY *is silent.*)

(*Worried by the silence.*) We're not *condemning* her, Mr Vining. (*Primly.*) It might happen to anyone. Laura was the kind of girl who wouldn't know any better.

(HENRY *is still silent.*)

SALLY (*to* EVELYN). He's angry with us. (*She crosses to* L. *of the table* R.C.) But we've known ever since she disappeared and we couldn't keep it back any longer.
EVELYN. No. He's not angry.
PHOEBE (*rising and moving down stage a little; to* EVELYN). You see, only three things could have happened to her: she's run away to hide; or she's thrown herself into the river; or it's him . . . (*Slowly.*) He committed a crime that night to cover everything up.
SALLY. We all knew that something would happen sometime.
PHOEBE (*after a pause; to* EVELYN). You won't think that it's just malicious gossip? We didn't come in that spirit at all.
EVELYN. No. We know that.
SALLY. It was when we started putting the bits and pieces together—they all fitted, you see.
PHOEBE. And there he was carrying on with his classes as if nothing had happened; when none of us could think about anything but Laura.
EVELYN (*rising*). We do appreciate, I'm sure. It's a blow to Mr Vining so don't blame him if he doesn't seem to take much notice. (*She crosses below the table and moves between* SALLY *and* PHOEBE.) I should go home now, if I were you; he's got a lot to think about.
PHOEBE. Yes. (*She turns to* HENRY.) Good night, Mr Vining.
EVELYN. Say good night, Henry.
HENRY. Good night.
SALLY. Good night, Mr Vining. (*She moves up to the hall door.*)
EVELYN. You know the way out, don't you, Sally?
SALLY. Yes, Miss Vining.

(*She exits to the hall.* PHOEBE *follows her off, shutting the door behind her.* HENRY *rises suddenly and bangs the arm of the chair.*)

EVELYN. They could be wrong.
HENRY. Their knowledge isn't wrong.
EVELYN. Don't fly into one of your rages.
HENRY. They're right in so much I know already they're likely to be right all through.
EVELYN. You think she's dead?
HENRY. I don't think—I just feel. He came here like some smooth counsel for his own defence; he talked me out of my doubts, my own instincts, and I believed him; he took me in as he took her in . . . (*He crosses deliberately to the table down* R.)
EVELYN. What are you going to do, Henry?
HENRY (*lifting the telephone receiver and dialling a number*). Take the first steps to wishing eternal damnation on him. (*Into the telephone.*) Inspector Garland . . .

The CURTAIN *falls*

ACT II

Scene 1

Scene.—*The sitting-room of the* Barlows' *house. Ten minutes later.*

When the Curtain *rises, the room is empty and the telephone is ringing.* Grace *enters. She looks pale and anxious. She hurries down* L. *to the telephone and lifts the receiver.*

Grace (*into the telephone*). Hullo . . . Mrs Barlow speaking . . . (*She listens for a moment, holding the receiver slightly away from her ear. Her mouth becomes set. Her face screws up as if she were listening to something acutely distasteful.*)

(Mrs Usher *appears anxiously at the door and watches* Grace Grace *quietly replaces the receiver.*)

Mrs Usher. Was that another of these calls?

Grace (*quietly*). Yes.

Mrs Usher (*coming down stage to the* L. *corner of the settee*). You shouldn't answer the phone, ma'am.

Grace. What can I do? I have to answer it. It might be the news we're waiting for.

Mrs Usher. Whatever news comes now will be bad.

Grace (*crossing down* R. *towards the easy chair ; a sharp edge to her voice*). Who are these people with their anonymous voices?

Mrs Usher. People with diseased minds, I'd say. Did it sound like the same man?

Grace. No, this time it was a woman. Sly—more filthy than the man.

Mrs Usher. You should complain to the operator.

Grace. I did last time. (*She moves below the settee.*) It was from a call-box.

Mrs Usher. You wouldn't think there could be such wicked people in the world.

Grace. Wouldn't you? I would. (*She sits on the settee,* R. *end.*)

Mrs Usher. I'd certainly get on to the operator again, ma'am.

Grace. No. She was on the side of the voices. I could tell from her manner when I said who I was. (*Bitterly.*) It appears I'm no longer in a position to lodge complaints.

Mrs Usher. You haven't done anything. Nobody could have anything to say against you. But once mud starts being flung about in this town nobody knows where to stop. (*She picks up the ashtray from the table behind the settee and crosses to the desk.*)

GRACE (*against her will*). Did you hear anything when you were out ? Anything fresh ?

(MRS USHER *empties the ashtray into the waste-paper basket and shakes her head evasively.*)

MRS USHER. No. Plenty of feelers going out though. Plenty of ferreting around to see what they can get out of me. Mrs Dinnage in the grocer's—not much time for people like me as a rule—but today you'd think we was thick as thieves.

GRACE. What did she want to know ?

MRS USHER (*crossing to the table behind the settee*). Just what was going on here. (*She replaces the ashtray.*)

GRACE. I hope you told her nothing was going on.

MRS USHER (*moving down* L. *of the settee*). She didn't get much change out of me, ma'am, don't worry. She tells me they're starting dragging the river, so I tell her it'll give the police something to do for a change—hauling up the old boots and broken bottles.

GRACE. Do they think the girl has committed suicide ?

MRS USHER (*after a slight hesitation; evasively*). I don't know, ma'am, what they think. Some of them think the worst, you can depend on that. (*She crosses down* R. *to the easy chair.*)

GRACE. What do you mean, the worst ? What could be worse than suicide, from everybody's point of view ?

(MRS USHER *picks up a newspaper from the easy chair.*)

MRS USHER. Well—she might have been done in. Interfered with, maybe, and then done in.

(GRACE *stares at* MRS USHER.)

GRACE. Who says that ?

MRS USHER. Gossip, ma'am, that's all. They don't know anything no more than we do. It's all coming from that school. Kids nowadays know too much for their own good. (*She crosses down stage, moves round the* L. *end of the settee and puts the newspaper on the table behind it.*)

GRACE (*tensely*). They think she might have—been waylaid —by some criminal ?

MRS USHER (*evasively*). Well—they don't think she went into the river of her own accord . . .

(GRACE *turns away.*)

That's to say if she is in the river.

(*The front door is heard to open and shut.* STEPHEN *appears in the hall, taking off his hat and coat.*)

Sc. 1]   THE DAY'S MISCHIEF   39

If that phone rings again, ma'am, let me answer it. (*She moves up stage* L. *of the door and stands holding it open*.)

(STEPHEN *goes out of sight for a moment to hang up his hat and coat, then enters and comes down to the back of the settee.* MRS USHER *exits, closing the door*.)

STEPHEN (*leaning over and kissing* GRACE *perfunctorily*). Hullo, darling. How are you?

GRACE. Waiting.

STEPHEN. Have you been out today?

GRACE (*with a shake of her head*). I can't. I feel as if there were a mob round the house.

STEPHEN. There isn't a soul anywhere near the house. (*He moves away* L. *of the settee*.)

GRACE. The town must be buzzing with rumour and gossip. People ring up . . .

STEPHEN (*turning; sharply*). Who rings up?

GRACE. People with no names—saying horrible things. (*Passionately*.) Why did we ever come to this town, Stephen? I never wanted to come. I hated it when we first stepped off the train a year ago. I had a horrible feeling about it . . . There was a voice over the loudspeaker at the station saying " Platform three for the London train—platform three for the London train " —just like that . . . It keeps going on in my head . . . I said to you then " Let's take it and go back to London."

STEPHEN. We'll be going back.

GRACE. What do you mean?

STEPHEN. I've been asked to resign. In fact I have resigned. (*He moves to the settee and sits on the* L. *arm*.)

(GRACE *stares at him in shocked silence*.)

GRACE (*in a low voice*). Where did that come from?

STEPHEN. Miss Faber.

GRACE. But she's always been so friendly. She knows us. She knows the kind of man you are. Look what she said last week when she came to dinner—how nice it was to come to a house like this, and talk. (*Anxiously*.) You remember? And we said afterwards it was one of the pleasantest evenings we had had since we came to Rudford.

STEPHEN. I know. But that was last week. (*He rises and moves away* L.)

GRACE (*urgently*). Well, tell me about it. What reasons did she give? She can't dismiss a man like you on rumours.

STEPHEN. She's been in close touch with the police. This afternoon I had a long session with her. (*Wearily*.) She was reasonable—and just. (*He turns back to* GRACE.) I see her point of view.

GRACE (*sharply*). What is her point of view?

STEPHEN (*hesitantly*). That ... Chiefly that there is no place for niceties of judgement in a relationship between a master and a girl pupil.
GRACE. But didn't you tell her there was no relationship?
STEPHEN. I could scarcely insist on that. The facts are against me. (*He crosses to the fireplace.*)
GRACE (*after a slight pause*). Didn't you put up any fight? Didn't you try to justify yourself? You know what a thing like this will do to your career. (*She rises and moves to him.*)
STEPHEN. Yes I know.
GRACE. Oh, darling, you must see a lawyer at once.
STEPHEN. Later. My career is not of first importance to me at the moment. I can think about that afterwards.
GRACE (*quietly and edgily*). Your concern is entirely for the girl?
STEPHEN (*gently*). Yes. Of course.

(GRACE *turns away and sits on the settee*, L. *end*.)

I've just been to see her father. I was able—I think—to put his mind at rest. At least I was able to convince him that I had done her no physical harm.
GRACE (*sharply*). Did he imagine you had?
STEPHEN. It's been three long days and nights. His mind is full of horrors. (*He moves in to her.*)
GRACE (*bitterly*). That isn't exclusive to him. Stephen, (*she pulls him down beside her*) if one could just for a moment penetrate this darkness of not-knowing. (*She looks at him. Quietly.*) Not knowing whether she is still in this world or not; and not knowing—I have to say this—your part in it.
STEPHEN. I've told you.
GRACE (*quietly*). What you told me didn't justify your being asked to resign. An innocent story that puts the affair in the class of an indiscretion.
STEPHEN. That kind of indiscretion gets one sacked from that kind of school.
GRACE. I don't want to harass you because I love you; but you've never told me the whole truth about that girl.
STEPHEN. I can't talk about it to you.
GRACE. Why not to me? I'm in this with you.
STEPHEN. I don't want you to be.
GRACE. We've no choice. We're here—immobilized in this room, with rumours and scandals and police activities going on outside. Our private life is in a state of suspense. The things outside may seem the larger issue to you but not to me.
STEPHEN. They're the same.
GRACE. Oh no! What I want to know is the inner meaning, because that is what concerns our marriage. A chance meeting with a girl on a road at night doesn't bring this—this injection

of drama into one's life. From what I know—and I only know what you've told me—it seems a monstrous injustice that you should be asked to resign. But you say no—Miss Faber was reasonable and just and you see her point of view.

STEPHEN. I do see it.

GRACE. I don't.

(STEPHEN *rises, moves up* R. *of the settee and crosses above it towards the desk.*)

STEPHEN. She made the point that if I met a girl pupil late at night on a lonely road why did I not see her safely back to her home. Why—that's to say—if I had a clear conscience.

(*There is a brief silence.*)

GRACE. What did you say?

STEPHEN. I said my conscience wasn't clear.

GRACE (*after a pause*). What does that mean?

STEPHEN. Just that I felt guilty enough to be reluctant to be seen with her at that hour, when only one interpretation would be put on it—a sexual one, let us face it.

GRACE. In what way guilty?

STEPHEN (*turning the desk chair and sitting in it*). Let's stop this now, Grace. I'm tired. I'm confused and distracted with worry.

GRACE. I too. That's why I can't let it rest. (*Very quietly.*) I feel as if I had been living on illusions. I've always been so sure that our marriage meant the same to you that it meant to me. I've never felt the need of children or friends or any kind of contact except you. I've even felt that life was too short. I've tried to bring myself to believe in another world only because I couldn't submit to separation from you.

(STEPHEN *stares at the floor. He is much moved. For a while there is silence. He rises and moves restlessly above the desk to the window.*)

(*Presently.*) Apart from you I've no independent existence. But you have, apart from me.

STEPHEN (*turning; gently*). It's a pity to attach unique importance to one person. It makes for rebellion in some form or other. One has, don't you see, to hold out for one's own stature—no less but certainly no more.

GRACE. I don't see.

STEPHEN. Unless one is to end up crippled by self-deception.

GRACE. You mean you rebelled against the closeness of our marriage? That sounds terribly like an excuse to me. An afterthought—to put part of the onus of all this on me.

(STEPHEN *crosses to the fireplace.*)

STEPHEN. I'd rather talk the language of facts, Grace. It was you who first mentioned the word love to the girl. You accused her of being in love with me. I don't think she knew it.
GRACE (*sharply*). That's the most childish thing I've ever heard you say.
STEPHEN. She didn't know it. I asked her.
GRACE (*angrily*). And then you both lied to each other like mad; dating your awareness of it from the moment I mentioned it—as if I had handed it to you on a plate. With my blessing no doubt!
STEPHEN (*quietly*). It wasn't like that at all.
GRACE (*still angry*). How was it then? You obviously talked of your love for each other . . . Did you tell the police that?

(STEPHEN *winces*.)

STEPHEN (*quietly*). Don't turn against me, Grace.

(GRACE *breaks down, weeping bitterly*. STEPHEN *moves to* R. *of her and sits on the settee, putting his arm gently across her shoulders. For a moment they don't speak*.)

GRACE (*hysterically*). I couldn't turn against you. And I couldn't live without you. I hope she's dead. (*She rises and moves* L. *towards the desk*.)
STEPHEN (*whipped into sudden anger*). Don't say that!
GRACE. I do say it. I hope she's dead and out of our lives.
STEPHEN (*stunned and cold*). If she's dead she'll never be out of our lives. The only hope of her being out of my life is that she is still alive.

(GRACE *takes this with numbed nerves; her face pale and drawn*.)

GRACE (*her manner almost casual*). You must love her very much.
STEPHEN (*slowly and thoughtfully*). I love her at the moment in the way one must love a child that is lost.
GRACE (*sitting in the desk chair; acid with the hurt*). Her disappearance is very clever. Well-timed too.
STEPHEN. Whatever happened it's without motive on her part. She had no tricks.
GRACE (*bitterly*). All innocence!
STEPHEN (*levelly*). There's little innocence in that generation.
GRACE (*immobile*). You found that out?
STEPHEN. I found a kind of despair that was more disturbing. The young—the intelligent young—seem to have a very much larger stake in the general malaise than we have.
GRACE (*cynically*). She seems to have achieved her effects. Built herself up into a *femme fatale* in the course of a single evening.
STEPHEN (*withdrawn*). We'd better not talk about her any

more. (*He rises, moves to the fireplace, and takes a cigarette from the box on the mantelpiece.*)

GRACE (*raising her voice*). But you love talking about her. You can't think or speak of anything else.

STEPHEN (*bursting out*). Naturally I can't! She has crossed my path with a vengeance. It has made me take stock of myself and my relation to you and the routine of our life. Of course I must think of her. (*He lights his cigarette.*)

GRACE (*with a trace of hysteria*). You love her. (*She rises and crosses to him.*) If she is found alive you'll leave me and go to her.

STEPHEN (*grimly*). All that I'm concerned with at the moment is that she should be found—alive.

GRACE (*solemnly*). Do you mean that?

STEPHEN. Of course I mean it.

GRACE (*after a moment's silence*). And if she isn't? What then?

STEPHEN (*after a pause*). I don't know.

GRACE. I can see no picture of her in my mind. I search and search but I can't visualize her or anything she may be doing. (*She moves down* R. *to the easy chair and sits.*) There are times when I forget my jealousy, Stephen. It lifts like a fog and I can see quite clearly. I know that I had a warning of this—a kind of prophetic warning. I've been uneasy for weeks and I didn't know why, until the girl stepped into the house that night. Then I knew. I brooded over it up in my bedroom, and when I came downstairs I behaved abominably. You said something about her crossing your path. I knew it before anything happened—while she was here in this room. I've been asking myself why. Which one of us is the plot directed against? Because I don't believe the paths of human beings cross by chance.

STEPHEN. Who can it be directed against except her—or me? Anyhow we shall soon know. They must find her very soon.

(MRS USHER *enters.*)

MRS USHER. Miss Faber to see you, sir.

(MISS FABER *enters quickly. She is a woman in her late forties; the headmistress of the school.*)

MISS FABER (*coming down stage* L. *of the settee*). Mr Barlow, I had to come and see you.

(MRS USHER *exits, shutting the door.*)

I'm very seriously disturbed. Good evening, Mrs Barlow. I thought it was better to come and see you than to try to talk to you on the telephone.

STEPHEN (*easing to the* R. *end of the settee*). I'm glad you came. Won't you sit down.

MISS FABER. Mr Barlow, after our talk this afternoon I found myself getting more and more uneasy . . . I can talk in front of your wife?
STEPHEN. Yes, of course.
MISS FABER (*moving below the* L. *end of the settee; to* GRACE). I don't think your husband realizes the seriousness of his position.
GRACE (*stiffly*). We both do, Miss Faber. (*She rises.*) It's a tremendously serious thing for my husband to be dismissed from the school.
MISS FABER. That was necessary. Nobody regrets it more than I do. But you see, as a woman in charge of a mixed school, I have no option. I have to keep the strictest discipline in matters that concern the tone and atmosphere of the school. From my point of view even a slight indiscretion is a serious matter. This was rather more than an indiscretion. (*She sits on the settee,* L. *end. To* STEPHEN.) You agree with me?
STEPHEN. Yes.

(GRACE *sits in the easy chair.*)

MISS FABER (*to* STEPHEN). I'm not given to dramatizing things, but if you knew how the school and the town are seething with rumour—one has to call it rumour because one is not yet in possession of all the facts—but if you knew the shape this story is taking our immediate worry wouldn't be your resignation.
STEPHEN. My immediate worry is the girl.
MISS FABER. She will be found if she is alive. But opinion inclines more and more to the view that she isn't.
GRACE. Public opinion?
MISS FABER. Police opinion too—I hate to say it. (*To* STEPHEN.) That's why I couldn't rest for thinking of you and your position. When we talked this afternoon I could see that you had no idea of its seriousness. Mr Barlow, I beg you to see your lawyer.
GRACE. About what?
STEPHEN. My lawyer is in London.
MISS FABER. Well, get him to come here. Explain the situation and ask his advice. I think it's most urgent.
GRACE (*rising and moving to* R. *of* MISS FABER). Miss Faber; you dismissed my husband on the one fact you know—that he had met this girl alone at night. The meeting was an accident. If he needs a lawyer it must surely be to discuss his position as regards the school and whether there is any redress against a decision like this.
STEPHEN (*crossing above the settee and coming down* L. *of it*). Grace; Miss Faber and I have already discussed this. The decision she took was inevitable. (*To* MISS FABER.) Please forgive my wife. The whole thing has been very worrying for her.

MISS FABER. I understand—and I'm very sorry. Believe me, Mrs Barlow, there was no malice in my having to ask your husband for his resignation. On the contrary ; I did it with the most genuine regret. The school will miss him very much. But I am responsible to the Ministry for the pupils under my care. (*To* STEPHEN.) Do you feel I treated you unjustly ?
    STEPHEN. No.
    GRACE (*wildly*). Then what is there in this that I don't know ?

(*There is a pause.*)

MISS FABER (*to* STEPHEN). If you were wise you would tell your wife the whole implications of this case.
    STEPHEN. I have tried to tell her. It's difficult. I don't want to involve my wife or to hurt her.
    MISS FABER. Naturally. But . . .
    GRACE. My husband is being victimized. He became the focus-point for an unhealthy adolescent infatuation. That is the whole root of the matter. Your responsibility in a mixed school should also extend to the people who have to teach these little horrors.
    MISS FABER (*quietly*). It does. If it had just been that it would have been easy. (*Gently.*) I don't think you know the facts and it is not my place to tell you. I wouldn't have begun this conversation if I hadn't thought you knew all about it.

(GRACE *turns away* R.)

STEPHEN (*to* GRACE). I didn't tell you, Grace, because I didn't think it would ever be necessary for you to know—but my meeting with Laura was not accidental. I telephoned her after she left here—she was alone—I asked her to meet me.
    GRACE (*blankly*). Oh.
    MISS FABER (*gently*). I thought she knew. I'm sorry. (*She looks at* GRACE. *Softly.*) My dear Mrs Barlow ; try to keep an open mind. You need one another's help at the moment more than anything else.

(GRACE *is silent.*)

(*She rises and moves to* STEPHEN. *Quietly.*) The police have already started dragging operations below the bridge. If they find her there your position will be pretty grim.
    STEPHEN. I realize that.
    MISS FABER. If I thought your association with Laura were some cheap little episode I should leave you to it. But I can't think it was.
    STEPHEN (*murmuring*). Thanks. (*He moves away* L.)
    MISS FABER. There's no valid law by which human beings can be assessed. (*With a slight deprecatory smile.*) Being the

type of woman I am, I have to assess men by their minds—it's all I know of them.

STEPHEN (*polite and embarrassed*). I assure you . . .

MISS FABER. Nevertheless you seem to be caught in a set of circumstances in which you are by no means blameless. I really urge you to organize some help for yourself.

GRACE. You think that if she is found dead, Stephen will be implicated?

MISS FABER (*guardedly*). If she is dead—there will be blame —I can't say to what extent.

STEPHEN. But, you think, to the extent of my having to defend myself on a charge?

MISS FABER. It's possible. Forgive my calling like this. Sitting alone in my house thinking over our conversation it seemed to me I might be able to do something to help. Goodbye, Mrs Barlow. (*She crosses to* GRACE.)

GRACE (*faintly*). Good-bye.

(STEPHEN *moves up stage and opens the door.*)

MISS FABER. I should like to keep in touch with you.

GRACE. Thank you.

(MISS FABER *crosses below the settee, moves up stage to the door and goes off* L. STEPHEN *follows her off. The front door is heard to shut.* STEPHEN *re-enters and shuts the door.*)

STEPHEN (*coming down stage and crossing below the settee to* GRACE). Grace—dear Grace—I didn't tell you because I didn't want to add to our trouble. I have kept some things back because I thought some solution to all this might have come by now.

GRACE. All I see is our whole life together collapsing around me.

STEPHEN. That isn't so. It's the same as it always was.

GRACE. Then you can have no idea of what it meant to me. (*She moves down* R. *to the easy chair.*)

STEPHEN. I've spoken about this affair in the *spirit* of the truth.

GRACE (*bitterly*). Truth? Suddenly we've been brought face to face with the extent of the pretence of our lives.

STEPHEN. There has been very little pretence in our lives.

GRACE (*deeply depressed*). Then that was the beginning. Your creeping out at night to keep an appointment with a girl of seventeen. Where does one go from there? Our life changes colour under our eyes.

STEPHEN. I met her that night but there was no motive . . .

(GRACE *shows no reaction.*)

(*He crosses* L. *to the window.*) I can't convince you. (*Bitterly.*)

And you have the advantage because you have caught me out in a lie.

GRACE. Can't you see that I'm terrified because of what I don't know ? One lie—one inaccuracy ; but how many more, Stephen ? What sort of mess are you in ? What's to happen to you—and to me ?

(MRS USHER *enters. She looks frightened and anxious, and closes the door behind her.*)

MRS USHER. It's the police again, sir. They want to talk to you.

(*There is a long tense silence.*)

STEPHEN. Where are they ? (*He moves up stage to* R. *of* MRS USHER.)

MRS USHER (*opening the door*). In the hall, sir.

(STEPHEN *exits and goes off* L. MRS USHER *follows him, leaving the door open.*)

POLICEMAN (*off*). Good evening, Mr Barlow.
STEPHEN (*off*). Good evening.
POLICEMAN (*off*). One or two points have cropped up which need more explanation. The Inspector would like you to come down to the station with me so that he can have a further talk with you. I suppose it's quite convenient for you to come at once ?

STEPHEN (*off*). Yes. Yes, of course. I'll tell my wife I'm going.

(*He enters and comes down stage to* GRACE.)

(*Very quietly.*) Darling ; I have to go to the station. More questions, but I don't suppose I shall be long.

(GRACE *stands looking at him transfixed.* STEPHEN *takes her in his arms but she is quite rigid.*)

Don't worry too much, my darling.

(*He moves quickly to the door and goes off* L. *The front door is heard to shut.* MRS USHER *enters. She leaves the door open.*)

MRS USHER. Are you all right, ma'am ?
GRACE. Yes, thank you.
MRS USHER (*coming down stage*). It doesn't mean it's an arrest, ma'am. It didn't look like that to me. They spoke very civil to him. Don't go and upset yourself, he wouldn't want you to. Is there something I could do ?
GRACE. No, thank you.
MRS USHER. It's a pity you haven't any friends here, or relations. Haven't you got anybody you can send for ?
GRACE. I haven't.

MRS USHER. It doesn't do for people to sit alone brooding about things.
GRACE. I prefer to be alone.
MRS USHER. You can have too much of it, ma'am. It doesn't do any good at a time like this.
(*The front-door bell rings.* MRS USHER *exits, closing the door. After a moment she re-enters.*)
It's a Miss Vining to see you, ma'am.
GRACE. I don't want to see anyone . . .

(EVELYN *enters.*)

EVELYN (*brushing past* MRS USHER). Thank you. (*She comes down* L. *of the settee.*) I knew you'd be alone. I live with my brother and his wife so I know all that is happening.

(MRS USHER *exits, shutting the door.*)

GRACE. If you knew I'd be alone, why did you come here?
EVELYN. I wanted to see you. It seemed silly that we should each be shut up by ourselves when there is so much to say.
GRACE. What is there to say?
EVELYN. A great deal that I can make clear to you.
GRACE. You look as if you are going to talk about the will of God.
EVELYN. I'm not qualified to speak for God.
GRACE. That's a change in this town.
EVELYN. It's an ignorant town. I live in it but I'm not of it, if you know what I mean. Neither are you I imagine?
GRACE (*withdrawn*). No.
EVELYN. I have an unusual mind that detects the pattern in lives. When one has that gift one doesn't stop at detecting; one must go on and impart one's knowledge. Do you follow what I mean?
GRACE. I'm afraid I'm very preoccupied, Miss Vining.
EVELYN. You knew my niece Laura?
GRACE (*coldly*). I met her once.
EVELYN. Laura was me. She sprang from commonplace parents—my brother and his wife; but her real kinship was with me. She had the same power to love. It is very rare.
GRACE (*with steady hostility*). Not nearly rare enough.
EVELYN. You say that out of your present pain. (*She moves deliberately below the settee and sits,* L. *end.*)
GRACE. Did you come here just to talk about her?
EVELYN. No. About you. No-one was giving a thought to you. It suddenly occurred to me how absolute your loneliness must be—now and in the future. Loneliness is something I understand.
GRACE. Miss Vining, please get to the point of this conversa-

tion. You may mean well but you've chosen a bad moment to come here. I don't want to see anyone and I don't know you.

EVELYN. Not yet, but our destinies are very closely linked. The same tragedy has struck our house and yours.

(GRACE *stares at her.*)

GRACE. The same misfortune, I would say.

EVELYN. I meant tragedy—with consequences that affect you even more than anyone else. That is why I came here—to try and help you. I know I don't know you except by sight. I have seen you often but never alone—always with him. You seemed inseparable. (*She takes her cigarette case from her bag, takes out a cigarette and lights it.*)

(GRACE *turns away.*)

Now you are separated.

GRACE. Don't let's become melodramatic, Miss Vining. My husband has gone to the police station, as you seem to know. I could scarcely go there with him.

EVELYN. The brave face is not necessary in front of me, because I don't see it—I see behind it. I know this sudden desperate blank in your life—the terrifying emptiness—I was faced with it many years ago.

GRACE (*detached*). I'm sorry. (*She turns to the fireplace.*)

EVELYN. Don't be sorry, because it was the beginning of a new life.

GRACE (*in the same tone*). I'm glad.

EVELYN. Now it's you who face that kind of crisis. I should be a miserable creature if I didn't try to help you. (*She rises as she speaks, moves in a businesslike manner round the* L. *end of the settee, takes the ashtray from the table behind it and returns to her seat.*) You are at the point of the pattern where you will either tear yourself to shreds or you will re-dedicate your life. Left to yourself you will think only in circles. You will work yourself into a state of agony which I can prevent.

GRACE (*turning to* EVELYN). I didn't think it possible to exaggerate this trouble we are in—but surely, Miss Vining, you. are exaggerating a little.

EVELYN. You haven't yet taken in what it means to be bereft of love—to be alone for ever.

GRACE (*with some impatience*). I'm very sorry if that has happened to you but . . .

EVELYN. Don't be sorry. No-one need ever be sorry for me. I am trying to tell you that love never deserts you. It identifies itself with every small thought and action in your daily life and then in sleep it shapes them into their real significance. It has been my special destiny to discover love triumphant and unchanging. You see how wrong you are when you say you are sorry for me.

GRACE (*more impatiently*). Yes. I see.

EVELYN. My real friends—the few people whom I call my friends—envy me.

GRACE. I'm sure.

EVELYN. Compare it with love in the flesh—married love—any love between man and woman—anxious, quarrelsome, sexual, treacherous.

GRACE (*crossing to* L. *of the settee ; more sharply*). Miss Vining, this obviously isn't nonsense to you but you must forgive me if I'm not capable of either listening to you or answering you at the moment.

EVELYN (*eagerly*). You think I talk nonsense, like my brother and his wife.

GRACE. I don't believe you or disbelieve you. (*Her voice rises in quick impatience.*) I don't care ! I've too much on my mind. All my thoughts are with my husband. (*She crosses to the fireplace.*)

EVELYN. Why ? His have not been with you.

GRACE (*turning to her*). I don't know if you are unbalanced or just impertinent.

EVELYN. Who is the judge of balance ? This evening during my brother Henry's outburst it was I who kept my balance. He yelled and shouted at the police, calling for eternal damnation on your husband. But my thoughts flew immediately to you and your future—in spite of my grief for Laura.

GRACE (*quiet and very frightened*). Grief ?

EVELYN. She is dead.

(GRACE *is silent, staring at* EVELYN *in fear.*)

GRACE (*presently*). When did you learn this ?

EVELYN. Just before I came here. I told you tragedy had struck both our homes.

(GRACE *sits in the easy chair. She is rigid with shock.*)

It is a shock for you. (*She rises.*) It won't be when you begin to see the purpose. There is always a purpose. (*She kneels beside* GRACE *and tries to take her hand.*)

(GRACE *withdraws her hand.*)

(*Softly.*) My hand seems to you like an intruder. (*She looks at her hand.*) Soon everything will seem different. It is the beginning of change from one world to another. (*She rises.*) You will rise to a higher level of love. From there you will see the physical level as it is with its lies, its infidelities and its violence.

(GRACE, *who has not been listening, appears to hear the word violence.*)

GRACE (*harshly*). Why did the police come for my husband?
EVELYN Don't you know? Why do you jib at violence when you have already accepted lies and infidelity?

(GRACE *stares at her in silence.*)

(*Presently.*) He killed her. Henry knows.

(GRACE *remains silent and rigid. When at last she moves it is to make a movement of utter distraction. She is unable to speak.*)

(*Presently.*) Henry was as distracted as you are. But he shouts. (*To herself. Gently.*) Henry has the mentality of a cavalry regiment. (*She turns away* L.)

GRACE (*suddenly looking at her*). You're insane. I'm almost as insane listening to you.

EVELYN (*amazed*). You talk like them. I will give you the cold facts and then you can judge if I am insane. Laura was pregnant. He must have made his escape from the holy edifice of marriage to look for love.

(GRACE *is struck silent again.*)

They have been meeting for months. Those long walks he took by the riverside—he was not alone. She was with him.

(GRACE *is still silent.*)

(*She puts her hand to her forehead and moves below the settee.*) I didn't mean to talk to you like this but you talk like my brother and his wife. You have the same pitiful arrogance about marriage. The great security! What have you got left when you find it was all an illusion? (*She sits on the settee.*)

(GRACE *looks at her for a moment in silence out of her anguish.*)

GRACE (*with difficulty*). You—wouldn't—lie—about—this?
EVELYN (*calmly*). I never lie. Ring up and ask Henry. Ring the police. Ask anyone in the town—they all know. Henry is the kind who shouts his private drama from the house-tops.

(GRACE *is trembling. She rises, goes to the door and opens it.*)

GRACE (*calling*). Mrs Usher. Mrs Usher.
MRS USHER (*off*). Yes, ma'am, I'm coming.

(MRS USHER *comes running in from off* R.)

GRACE (*pleading; hysterically*). Mrs Usher, is there any truth in what she tells me? (*She pulls* MRS USHER *down stage to* L.C.)
MRS USHER (*to* EVELYN). What have you been telling her? Mr Barlow said she must *not* be worried. I knew by the look of you I should never have let you in here. (*To* GRACE.) But she would come in, ma'am.

GRACE (*to* MRS USHER). Is it true that the girl was pregnant? The truth please—I *must* know.

(MRS USHER *doesn't want to answer.*)

(*Wildly.*) Those telephone calls? Is that what they meant? (*She breaks down and collapses in the desk chair.*)

(MRS USHER *is stumped.*)

MRS USHER (*turning fiercely on* EVELYN). What did you want to come here for? She would have heard in God's good time—the proper way—from people who knew how to break it to her. Look at the state you've got her into, you interfering bitch. Get out! Come on, get out!

(EVELYN *rises, moves round the* L. *end of the settee and makes an unhurried exit. She goes off* L. MRS USHER *follows her to the door and shuts it after her. She comes down* R. *of* GRACE.)

(*Gently.*) That girl must have led him on, ma'am. It was you he loved, there was never a shadow of a doubt about that.

(GRACE *is immobile as a statue, her eyes staring and fixed.*)

I'll swear before the whole world it was you he loved. If he's thrown the little slut into the river it's where she belongs and good riddance to her, coming between a man and his wife. If there's any justice in the land they'll let him off.

(GRACE *doesn't move.*)

I should have told you before, ma'am. The police were here this morning to take away the clothes he wore that night. Somebody should have prepared you, but Mr Barlow asked me not to tell you. He was thinking about you up to the last. (*She begins to cry.*) When they took him away just now he said to me " Look after her, Mrs Usher ; she's lonely " he said.

(GRACE *rises and crosses slowly below the settee.*)

(*Presently.*) Would you like me to fetch the doctor, ma'am? It's a terrible shock.

GRACE. No thanks. Just leave me, will you.

(MRS USHER *is unwilling to go.*)

(*To herself.*) Is it possible? It *is* possible, isn't it? He would have seen it as more than he could face up to. There would have been me to tell—the school—and everything.

MRS USHER. Please let me fetch the doctor, ma'am. (*She moves towards* GRACE.) He would give you something.

(GRACE *shakes her head.*)

GRACE (*presently; with a bitter tragic smile*). What for?

Mrs Usher. I'll stay by you, ma'am, and see you through everything that's to come.
Grace. Through what?
Mrs Usher. He'll need you.
Grace. He won't. (*She looks round the room like a tragic lost creature, with a growing wildness.*)
Mrs Usher. Oh, ma'am, it's hard!

(Grace *does not appear to hear her.*)

Grace (*to herself*). The light of his presence . . . (*To* Mrs Usher; *with a helpless smile.*) Do you see what I mean?
Mrs Usher. I've got to get the doctor. I'm going to bring him straight back with me. I shan't be a few minutes.

(*She exits, closing the door behind her.* Grace *stands immobile. After a moment the front door is heard to close. The telephone rings.* Grace *turns her eyes to the instrument and stares at it while it continues ringing. After a while she crosses down* L. *and lifts the receiver to her ear. She doesn't say a word, but the wildness of her emotion increases as she listens. She puts the receiver down, standing quite still. She is now in a state; she looks trapped in the room. She hurries to the door, opens it quickly and moves into the hall. She throws a coat round her shoulders and hurries out* L.)

Quick Curtain

Scene 2

Scene.—*The living-room of the* Vinings' *house. Three hours later.*

When the Curtain *rises,* Evelyn *is sitting above the table* R.C. *darning socks. On the table is a work-basket.* Henry *enters from off* L. *by the garden door. He is dishevelled and haggard, his shoes are muddy and he wears a wet mackintosh. He shuts the door behind him, comes down* C. *and throws himself exhausted on the settee. For a while there is silence.*

Evelyn (*presently*). Have you been down to the river again?
Henry. Yes. (*Again he is silent. Abstractedly.*) Give me a drink, Evelyn, please.

(Evelyn *rises and moves down* R. *to the table.*)

No water.

(Evelyn *pours out a whisky, and takes it to him.*)

It's like standing at the gates of Death searching amongst the people going in for the face you know. Thanks. (*He takes the*

glass. *Physically and emotionally he is all in, and he covers his face with his free hand.*)
EVELYN. Hadn't you better take off that damp coat?
(HENRY *does not appear to have heard.*)
Are your feet wet?
(HENRY *is still silent. Presently he looks up.*)
HENRY. How's Vi? (*He empties his glass.*)
EVELYN. I've been trying to get her to take a hot bath, but she won't. She won't even wash. She won't do anything. (*She takes his glass, crosses down.* R. *to the table and puts it down, moves above the table* R.C. *and sits.*)
HENRY. I'd better go and see how she is. (*He rises and moves round the* R. *end of the settee, taking off his coat. He puts it on the table up* L. *and moves towards the hall door.*)

(VI *enters from the hall. She is wan and untidy, still in her old dressing-gown.*)

VI. Is there any news?
HENRY (*moving to her and putting an arm round her shoulder; very tenderly*). Nothing new, my darling. Have you slept?
VI. No.
HENRY. Come and sit down by me.

(*He leads* VI *down to the settee and they sit,* HENRY *at the* R. *end,* VI *at the* L. *He takes her hand in his.* EVELYN'S *eyes never leave them.*)

(*Quietly; not looking at* VI.) It may be we shall only have each other—but at that we shan't be utterly lost.

(*In silence* HENRY *and* VI *both stare ahead, almost past feeling.*)

EVELYN. Why don't you put on a pair of dry socks, Henry? I've been darning some for you.
VI (*to* HENRY). Will you be going out again?
HENRY (*gently*). Not if you want me to stay in.
VI. Don't go out, Henry.

(HENRY *strokes her hand.*)

HENRY. Have you had anything to eat?
EVELYN (*crisply*). She hasn't eaten a thing all day.
HENRY. She must. (*To* VI.) You must, my love. (*To* EVELYN.) Go and get her something, Evelyn.

(EVELYN *rises, a strange smile on her face.*)

EVELYN (*moving up to the hall door*). Go and be a drudge, Evelyn—you who have no heart, no mind, no soul.
HENRY (*his nerves snapping*). What on earth is all that about?

EVELYN (*opening the door*). I mean that I who know nothing about human love or passion can do the household chores.
(*She exits, the same smile on her face.*)
VI. She's talked about nothing but love all day. Highfalutin talk that drives one silly. She went to see Mrs Barlow.
HENRY (*frowning*). Tonight?
VI (*wearily*). Yes. She went out soon after you.
HENRY. Why tonight? What did she want to butt in there for?
VI. I don't know.
(HENRY *thinks this over for a moment.*)
HENRY. What in heaven's name could she have had to say to her?
VI. She didn't tell me.
HENRY. I'd better go and have a word with her.
(*He rises and exits to the hall. He leaves the door open.* VI *is scarcely aware he has gone. She puts her feet up on the settee and closes her eyes in utter exhaustion. After a moment the garden door opens quietly and* LAURA, *wet, pale, frightened and unsure of herself, stands in the doorway. She sees the back of her mother's head, and stands looking at it—a faint nervous smile coming over her face. She shuts the door and comes quietly down* R. *of the settee.*)
LAURA (*in a whisper*). Mother . . . (*She stands looking at* VI *over the end of the settee.*)
(*Slowly* VI *becomes aware of someone. Her eyes open and she stares at* LAURA. LAURA *moves quickly below the settee and throws herself into* VI'S *arms. There are no words, only the mother's clutching arms and their mingled sobs. Presently* VI *sits up. She kisses* LAURA'S *face all over.*)
VI (*in tears, between kisses*). My darling! My baby! (*Calling.*) Henry.
LAURA (*weeping*). Mother, you look so ill! I didn't mean to hurt you.
VI (*embracing her again*). Oh, my baby! We thought you were dead. (*Calling.*) Henry. It's Laura. Laura's back. (*She is a little hysterical, as she laughs and weeps and clutches* LAURA *to her breast.*)
(HENRY *enters from the hall. He stops dead just inside the doorway and stares at them, motionless with shock.*)
HENRY (*in a strange, uncertain voice*). Laura . . . ?
(LAURA *rises and crosses slowly to* HENRY. *She stops a few paces from him.*)

LAURA (*uncertainly*). Daddy . . . Are you very angry?

(*They move towards each other and* HENRY *takes her in his arms. His face twists with emotion. In his exhaustion a sharp intake of breath tells us how near he is to breaking-point.*)

HENRY. We thought we'd never see you again. Let us thank God, Vi, for taking us out of our darkness.

VI. I do, Henry. I do. Oh, my darling, it's been so awful! (*She rises and moves to* L. *of* LAURA.) We've been in such a state. I've never stopped crying, have I, Henry? I cried so much—I don't know any more.

HENRY. She's even stopped talking, believe it or not.

LAURA. Oh, Mother!

VI. They've been giving me drugs to make me sleep, that's why I look so terrible. I didn't care.

HENRY. She's been wandering about like a ghost. (*He releases* LAURA.)

VI. If I'd known I'd have tidied myself up. But I didn't care, you see.

HENRY. It doesn't matter.

VI. Oh, baby, where have you been? (*She hugs* LAURA.)

HENRY. No questions, Vi, no reproaches. She's home.

LAURA. Mother, you look so ill! (*She turns to* HENRY.) Daddy, I'm so sorry. (*She weeps on his shoulder.*)

HENRY (*putting an arm round her; gently*). My darling, we go through these crises in our lives and they're truly terrible.

LAURA. But you and mother . . . You both look so worn-out! How could I have done this to you?

VI. Don't worry about us. We're all right. God is good. And I've been saying such wicked things about Him in my heart . . . (*She feels* LAURA'S *clothes.*)

HENRY. He'll forgive you.

VI. You're so cold, baby! Take that coat off.

(LAURA *takes off her coat.* VI *helps her and hands it to* HENRY *who moves up* L. *and puts it on the table with his own.*)

They've been giving me things to make me sleep and I'm all mixed up with them. (*She leads* LAURA *below the settee to the fireplace.*)

(EVELYN *enters from the hall. She remains by the door.*)

EVELYN. I heard voices. I couldn't believe my ears.

VI. Look at her, Evelyn. My baby—my little girl—all safe and sound.

EVELYN (*to* LAURA). We thought you were dead. (*To* HENRY.) You said she was.

HENRY (*coming down to the* R. *end of the settee*). Yes. It doesn't matter any more what we thought. She's here.

(EVELYN *stands looking at them.*)

VI (*hugging* LAURA). Oh, my darling!
EVELYN (*muttering*). I made a mistake ...
VI (*catching sight of* EVELYN ; *emotionally*). Evelyn, what's the matter with you? You love her too—don't you care that she's back?

(EVELYN *turns and exits to the hall.*)

Come and sit down and get warm. The police have been dragging the river for you.
LAURA. The police?
VI. They've been looking everywhere for you.

(HENRY *crosses down* R. *to the telephone and dials a number.*)

Everybody's been looking for you except me. And they've been filling me so full of drugs that I don't know if this is true or not.
HENRY (*into the telephone*). Inspector Garland, please ...
LAURA. Oh, Mother, I'm so sorry.
HENRY (*into the telephone*). Bob? ... Henry Vining here. Laura's back ...
VI. Daddy won't let me ask you too many questions, but there's a hundred things I must know ...
HENRY (*into the telephone*). Yes, a few minutes ago ... Yes, safe and well ...
LAURA. I'll tell you tomorrow, darling. There's nothing very important to tell ...
HENRY (*into the telephone*). I just wanted you to know. I'll be along to see you later. (*He replaces the receiver and moves above the table* R.C.)
VI. Tomorrow I'll be able to listen. Are you hungry?
LAURA (*half-laughing, half-crying*). Yes.
VI. I'll get you something to eat. (*She crosses to* HENRY.) I'm all right again, Henry. I'm alive again.

(LAURA *moves below the settee to the* R. *end.*)

(*To* LAURA.) You see they've been giving me things to make me sleep and I'm a bit mixed up. (*She kisses* LAURA.) I won't be a minute.

(*She exits to the hall.*)

HENRY (*moving down* R. *to the table*). She hardly knows what she's doing.
LAURA. Daddy, she looks so ill!
HENRY. Well, we've been worried. She'll be all right now you're home. (*He pours out a drink.*)

(LAURA *moves away in silence below the settee.*)

LAURA (*softly*). I'm so ashamed. I don't know what to say to you. (*She sits on the settee,* L. *end.*)
HENRY (*crossing to* LAURA *with the drink*). Here, drink this up. It's neat.
LAURA (*looking at the drink*). I'd be sick.
HENRY. No you won't. It'll do you good ; stop you shaking.
(LAURA *takes the drink and swallows it.* HENRY *moves up to the hall door and shuts it. He comes down to the table* R.C.)
(*Quietly.*) Laura, I want to ask you one question straight and then no more. They say you ran away because you were going to have a baby.

(LAURA *stares at* HENRY *wide-eyed and solemn.*)

LAURA (*presently; in a whisper*). Me?
HENRY. If it's true don't be afraid to tell me.
LAURA (*after a shocked silence*). No! No; it's *so* wrong! It's so *far* from the truth. Me? Who said so? Who even *thought* of it?
HENRY. Good. Now let's forget it for ever. (*He moves down* R. *to the table and pours himself a drink.*)
LAURA (*following* HENRY *thoughtfully with her eyes; quietly*). Do you want to know *why* I ran away?
HENRY. I know enough. Don't let's talk about it. (*He crosses to the settee and sits* R. *of* LAURA.) Where did you go?
LAURA. London. A girl I know there helped me. I owe her two pounds.
HENRY. Tell me about her later and we'll see to it.
LAURA (*softly*). I was going to stay away until I had worked things out in my mind. But then I thought you and mother might be getting anxious.
HENRY. Yes—we were—a little.
LAURA. What's this about the police?
HENRY. Nothing. Routine stuff. We had to report you missing.
LAURA. But I've only been away three days.
HENRY. Three days can be quite a long time.
LAURA. I'll never do it again. (*She looks at* HENRY.) I was in a state. I didn't think. Life is very difficult, isn't it?
HENRY. Very.
LAURA. I was desperately unhappy—and muddled.
HENRY. One is at times. One goes into the wilderness.
LAURA. Yes.
HENRY. One tries to reach the last line of the sonnet.
LAURA (*softly*). The truth, you mean?

(HENRY *nods.*)

(*After a moment's thought.*) But when the truth is something you can't bring yourself to face . . .

Sc. 2]   THE DAY'S MISCHIEF

HENRY (*gently*). Then you've got to fortify yourself to face it.
LAURA. I did. I know what I have to do. I have to forget him. (*She rises and moves to the fireplace. She puts her glass on the mantelpiece and stands with her back to* HENRY.)
HENRY. That's too glib, my darling.
LAURA (*after a brief silence*). Daddy; have you seen him?
HENRY. Yes. He's been in a spot of trouble.
LAURA (*anxiously*). Trouble?
HENRY. He'll be all right now. But you . . . You're still left with the problem, aren't you? You're still in love with him.

(LAURA *doesn't look at him or answer*.)

He loves his wife.
LAURA. I know.
HENRY (*slowly; feeling his way*). Laura, I don't quite know how to tackle this. From its very secretness and inwardness love is not easy to talk about. But you're my child and I hate to see this—this distress—go on.
LAURA (*not looking at him; without much conviction*). I have to get over it, I know. I will.
HENRY (*anxiously*). And quickly, my darling. But how?

(LAURA *is silent*. HENRY *rises and moves thoughtfully towards the hall door*.)

What should I say to you? Perhaps I'm the wrong person to attempt it. My contribution to the high passions is a very small one. I fell in love with your mother, I married her and lived happily—that's all.

(LAURA *sits on the settee*, L. *end*.)

But because I found love in my own back-garden it doesn't blind me to the fact of the jungle outside. I know that love drives people to prisons—to churches—to the gallows—asylums—to their graves. (*He turns to* LAURA.) I can't laugh at this turmoil of first love—not after the anxieties of these last three days—I can't try to chivvy you out of it—I can't offer you cynicisms because I have a soul and you have a soul. (*Firmly*.) So how do we treat this episode? Let us have no stiff-upper-lip nonsense at all costs. Let's face it as it is—love misplaced, love incomplete, love to which you have no right whatsoever. (*He moves below the settee to her. Gently*.) And let us rely on your own dignity of mind to see you out of it. (*With a slight smile*.) Does all that seem just a torrent of words to you? (*He sits on the settee*, R. *of* LAURA.)
LAURA. No.
HENRY. There's something else I'd like to say to you. You see there are two ways of looking at life. To the common sense all things are ordinary, but perceived by the imagination they are

extraordinary and unique. It is worth while to make some effort to strike a balance between the two. I say this with your Aunt Evelyn in mind. You may not see the connection but she has leapt forward in my consciousness these last three days.

LAURA (*puzzled*). Evelyn?

HENRY. Yes. She's your nearest example of the twists that extravagant emotions can take.

LAURA. But she's old.

HENRY. She wasn't always old. And she had something—a great depth of affection, a power to love. She's become a family joke—but she isn't a joke. (*He rises and crosses to the fireplace.*) Her arid destiny is not a joke either. There must be a great many people whose lives are determined by their first experience of love.

LAURA. Why are you talking about her?

HENRY (*turning to* LAURA ; *sitting on the fender*). A warning, that's all. The imagination can turn substance into shadow and vice versa. It's a question of how the light falls.

LAURA. Do you mean her crushes on other women?

HENRY. I mean her compensations—her efforts to free herself from her own alone-ness. (*Conversationally.*) She *was* young, you know—and pretty—and attractive. She had a love affair that went wrong and she wouldn't let go. She clung to it—she stored it up.

LAURA (*with a slight smile*). Do you see me like Evelyn in thirty years' time?

HENRY (*smiling*). I can't see that. I've been thinking too much—worrying too much. Every bush has been a bear. It doesn't arise. Her affair came to a disastrous end. This hasn't, thank heaven. (*He rises, crosses to the table* R.C. *and sits above it.*)

LAURA (*quietly*). It has just come to an end.

HENRY. Yes.

LAURA (*after a moment's silence*). Daddy, when you said he had been in trouble . . . (*She rises and moves to* HENRY.) How much trouble?

HENRY (*hesitantly*). Well—in the first place his story was not believed.

LAURA. What did he say?

HENRY. What happened that night. Did he telephone you?

LAURA. Yes; to meet him. I met him and he talked to me. He tried to make me see . . . (*She stops, unable to tell more.*)

HENRY. Then he sent you home on the bus?

LAURA. Yes. But I didn't go . . . I ran back to find him but he had gone.

HENRY. Had you ever met him on that road before?

LAURA (*hesitantly*). No . . . I had seen him.

HENRY. Without his knowing you were there?

LAURA. He didn't know.

HENRY (*after a moment's thought*). That is what he said. I didn't believe him nor did anyone else. He has been considerably slandered.

LAURA. Oh, Daddy! (*She stares at him in astonishment and fear.*)

HENRY. As we've faced a few facts, my darling, let us face the rest. He has been under suspicion from the police; he has been persecuted by his pupils; and he has been asked to resign. You'll learn this sooner or later—you might as well hear it from me.

(LAURA, *utterly shocked, turns away.*)

Don't let it distress you too much. It can be put right. The pendulum will swing the other way when the injustice is made clear.

LAURA (*very tense*). I'd have died sooner than hurt him.

HENRY (*drily*). No doubt. (*He rises, and looks down at* LAURA.) Forget it. I shall see that it is put right. (*He pats her arm.*)

LAURA (*tensely*). You're sure?

(VI *enters from the hall. Her hair is tidy and she has put on a dress. She carries a tray of food.*)

VI (*coming down to the table* R.C.). There, love, some nice scrambled eggs on toast, and some hot coffee. (*She puts the tray on the table.*)

(LAURA *hastily wipes her eyes.* VI *looks from* LAURA *to* HENRY. HENRY *turns away guiltily.*)

(*Sharply.*) What have you been saying to her, Henry? (*She crosses to* LAURA *and leads her to the table* R.C.) Don't pay any heed to him, baby; he just likes to talk. Any chance to talk and he's there (*with a look at* HENRY) with all the things he's been writing in his columns that day.

HENRY (*quietly*). Vi dear . . .

VI. Don't give me any of it. She's back, that's all I care about. Eat this while it's hot, love.

(LAURA *sits above the table and picks up the knife and fork. The front-door bell rings.* HENRY *starts for the hall door.*)

(*She forestalls him.*) I'll go, Henry. It'll be people who have heard that Laura's back.

(*She exits to the hall, leaving the door open.* HENRY *crosses up stage to* R. *of* LAURA.)

(*Off.*) Oh, Mr Barlow! She's back home.

STEPHEN (*off*). Yes, I know. They told me.

(LAURA *puts down her knife and fork. She rises and stands tense and rigid.* HENRY *pats her arm and moves down* R. LAURA *crosses* L., *below the settee.* HENRY *glances at her.* VI *enters followed by* STEPHEN.)

VI (*happily*). We're so excited we hardly know what we're doing. Do come in. (*She moves up* L.) Damp coats all over the place.

(STEPHEN *comes down* C. LAURA *turns to face him.* VI *quietly picks up the two coats.*)

STEPHEN (*quietly*). Laura! How wonderful! And you're all right?

LAURA (*still numb*). Yes, thank you.

STEPHEN. We've been so anxious.

LAURA (*tense and stiff*). I know. I'm very sorry.

STEPHEN (*turning rather awkwardly to* HENRY). When they told me I couldn't believe them. (*He crosses to* HENRY. *Self-consciously.*) It takes some time to get used to it.

HENRY. Forgive me, won't you, for all my doubts.

STEPHEN (*quietly*). You were entitled to them.

HENRY. I should have recognized truth when I saw it.

STEPHEN (*with a smile*). I'm not holding it against you.

VI (*moving* C. *with the coats*). Henry, give Mr Barlow a drink. We'll all have a drink.

HENRY. Vi dear, some more glasses.

STEPHEN. Please don't trouble, Mrs Vining. (*He moves above the table* R.C.) I'm on my way home. My wife doesn't know the good news yet.

HENRY. Why don't you ring her up?

STEPHEN (*rather shyly*). I'd rather go and tell her.

VI. You must have a drink first.

(*She goes bustling out to the hall.*)

HENRY (*to* STEPHEN). Well, just one! I think we need it.

(STEPHEN *looks at* LAURA. *He moves towards her,* L. *of the table* R.C.)

STEPHEN (*with a tender smile*). Do you know the ballad of Bonnie Kilmeny?

LAURA. No.

STEPHEN (*quoting*). " Late, late in the gloamin' Kilmeny came hame." I think she must have looked rather like you.

HENRY (*casually*). She learned something in her wanderings, didn't she, Kilmeny?

STEPHEN. I don't remember.

HENRY. If she had any sense she did.

LAURA (*in a quiet, tense voice*). I'm very sorry for all the trouble I've caused you—and your wife.

STEPHEN (*to* LAURA; *gravely*). You walked away in an opposite direction. There is no need to apologize for that.

(LAURA *looks at him wide-eyed.* VI *enters from the hall with four glasses on a tray.* HENRY *moves up stage to meet her and takes the tray and glasses down* R. *to the table.*)

VI. Do you know, Mr Barlow, I was lying on the sofa with my eyes closed when I felt someone beside me—and there she was. (*She moves to* R. *of* STEPHEN.) We haven't even asked her yet where she's been. Now I've started to talk I can't stop.

HENRY. Vi dear, do you . . . ?

VI. If I have one drop of whisky it will go straight to my head but I don't care.

HENRY. Vi dear, I'm trying to ask Mr Barlow whether he takes water or soda?

STEPHEN. Water, please.

VI. One thing I'll never be is a drug addict. (*She crosses to* HENRY.) They've been giving me sleeping tablets and they've had every mortal effect on me except make me sleep.

(HENRY *holds out a glass to* VI.)

(*She takes the glass from* HENRY *and crosses to* STEPHEN.) There. (*She gives him the glass.*) Do you know, Mr Barlow, that . . .

HENRY. I don't think you should have one, Vi.

VI. He's afraid that if I have anything to drink I'll talk more and he won't be able to get a word in edgeways. Henry doesn't like anybody to talk except himself. But you see I . . .

HENRY (*with a benevolent shout*). Calm down. Pipe down. (*More quietly.*) Vi dear, go and sit beside your daughter and rest your nerves.

(VI *crosses to the settee and sits at the* R. *end.* LAURA *sits at the* L. *end.*)

STEPHEN (*smiling; quietly*). Well; here's to the happy ending. (*He drinks.*)

HENRY. Whatever harm has been done to you will be undone, I assure you.

STEPHEN. Those things sort themselves out.

(*The telephone rings.* HENRY *lifts the receiver.*)

HENRY (*into the telephone*). Yes . . . Speaking . . .

VI. Isn't it wonderful not to be paralysed with fright every time the phone rings?

STEPHEN. Yes.

HENRY (*into the telephone*). Yes . . .

STEPHEN. Will you forgive me if I knock this back quickly? I must get home to my wife. (*He drinks.*)

VI. Of course you must.

HENRY (*into the telephone*). What!
VI. Henry would keep you drinking and talking here all night, Mr Barlow.
STEPHEN. Not this night. I've been at the police station for about three hours. She'll be wondering what on earth I'm up to.
VI. Yes, she'll be worried.
HENRY (*into the telephone*). I can't, man . . . No I can't . . . Yes. (*He replaces the receiver.*)
VI. Who was it, Henry?

(HENRY *turns to* STEPHEN *but is unable to look at him. When he speaks his voice is strange and unnatural.*)

HENRY (*hesitantly*). It's—the—police. They're sending a car to take you home.
STEPHEN. I don't want their car. I don't want to go back to my wife in a police car. She's seen enough of them. (*He puts his glass down quickly on the table* R.C.) I must go before they come. (*He crosses to* VI, *holding out his hand.*) Forgive me for hurrying off, Mrs Vining. But I want to be the first to tell her that all is well. (*He shakes hands with* VI.) Good-bye, Laura.
LAURA (*with a faint smile*). Good-bye.
STEPHEN (*moving* C.; *to* HENRY). Tell them when they come that I've gone home. And will they please leave us alone.

(*He exits quickly to the hall.*)

VI. Laura, what about that food? You haven't touched a thing.
LAURA. I couldn't.
STEPHEN (*off*). Good night, Miss Vining.
EVELYN (*off*). Good night, Mr Barlow.
VI (*to* LAURA). What you need is a nice long sleep. That's what we all need. All we have to do is put our heads on our pillows and that's all we . . .

(EVELYN *enters from the hall.*)

EVELYN (*entering*). He left in a hurry. (*She comes* C.)
VI. He wanted to let his wife know. Have you put Laura's hot-water bottle in . . .
HENRY. What he doesn't know is that his wife is dead.

(*There is a shocked silence.* LAURA *rises.*)

They found a body in the river all right—but it was hers. (*He moves towards* EVELYN.) What did you say to her? What have we done to her? What sort of people are we?
VI (*rising and moving to* L. *of* EVELYN). Henry, be careful what you say. Please be careful. You'll say things you may never be able to take back.
HENRY. I couldn't tell him. I must go after him.

(*He exits quickly to the hall.*)

V1 (*following* HENRY). You must bring him back here . . .

(*She exits to the hall.*)

EVELYN. You're thinking you'll have to live with this for the rest of your life.

LAURA (*moving below the* R. *end of the settee; on the verge of hysteria*). I am to blame. I did it.

EVELYN (*moving to* LAURA). It's cruel, darling. A cruel way to lose him.

LAURA (*not listening*). I drove her to it. I was the cause of it.

EVELYN. Her tragedy is nothing to yours. (*She tries to put her arm round* LAURA.)

LAURA (*turning away*). What have I done? What do I do? How can I live? (*She breaks down and covers her face with her hands.*)

EVELYN (*turning* LAURA *to her bosom*). My darling, we'll find a way. Other people will try to make a lesson out of it; I can understand and guide you. You need me, Laura; and here I am, my whole life has been directed towards this moment.

LAURA (*crying hysterically*). Oh, Evelyn! Evelyn!

EVELYN. I am your refuge and your strength. Hush. Hush.

(HENRY *enters from the hall. He is followed by* V1. *He moves quickly to* R. *of* EVELYN *and pulls her away from* LAURA, *passing her across to* L. *of the table* R.C.)

HENRY. Laura, listen to me; Mr Barlow sent you a message: he said "Don't let there be any sense of blame or self-accusation in that child." He said "The causes were private; they were between my wife and myself, they had nothing to do with Laura." Now go into the kitchen and fetch me some water; I want a drink.

(LAURA *exits slowly to the hall.*)

(*He turns to* EVELYN.) Evelyn my dear, you must find yourself somewhere to live. Immediately. We are going to have a few difficult weeks with that child. I want to handle it myself. I hate to seem harsh, but I must insist on this.

(EVELYN *moves above the table* R.C. *and collects the work-basket and socks. She leaves one sock on the table.*)

EVELYN. I'll go now—tonight. I have friends—lots of friends.

V1 (*moving to* R. *of* HENRY). Henry, she doesn't have to go tonight.

(EVELYN *crosses above* V1 *and* HENRY *to the table up* L. *with the work-basket.*)

HENRY (*moving above the table* R.C.). She doesn't have to; but as she says—she has friends.

(LAURA *enters from the hall with a jug of water. She moves* L. *of* HENRY. EVELYN *tidies the work-basket.*)

(*He takes the jug.*) You'd better go to bed, my darling. Give her one of your sleeping tablets, Vi.

VI (*moving* L. *of* LAURA). Yes, I will.

HENRY. That will give you the good sleep you need. Tomorrow (*he moves down* R. *to the table and pours himself a drink*) we'll look things squarely in the face; call ourselves to the bar of our own reason.

VI (*urging* LAURA *to the door*). I'll follow you in a minute, love.

(LAURA *exits to the hall.*)

(*She moves down* R. *to* HENRY.) Henry, Mr Barlow never said that. He never sent any message; he could scarcely speak.

HENRY (*pausing, jug in hand*). No. But it's what he would have said.

VI. I see.

(*She exits to the hall.* HENRY *is engrossed pouring out his drink.* EVELYN *moves above the table* R.C. *with the work-basket and picks up the remaining sock.* HENRY *raises his glass to his lips.* EVELYN *looks at him.*)

EVELYN. I pity you, Henry, trying to play at God with a whisky glass in your hand.

(*She exits quickly to the hall.*)

CURTAIN

NOTE ON THE SETTINGS

ALTHOUGH all the essential features have been retained, the settings described in this Acting Edition represent a simplification of those used in the London Production. Reference to the dotted lines on the Ground Plans will show how it is only necessary for one side of each set to be struck. During the playing of the scenes in the Barlows' room the right side of the Vinings' set can remain standing with the furniture in the dining recess in place: while during the scenes in the Vinings' room the left side of the Barlows' room can remain, together with the desk and chair. With the aid of loose covers (for the Barlows' room) the same settee and easy chair can be used in both scenes; also the table behind the Barlows' settee, which is not seen by the audience, can do service as the table down R. in the Vinings' room. If further simplification should be called for, the dining recess could be cut out; it is not essential to the action of the play, though there would be some loss to the character of the room.

FURNITURE AND PROPERTY PLOT

ACT I

SCENE 1

The BARLOWS' room

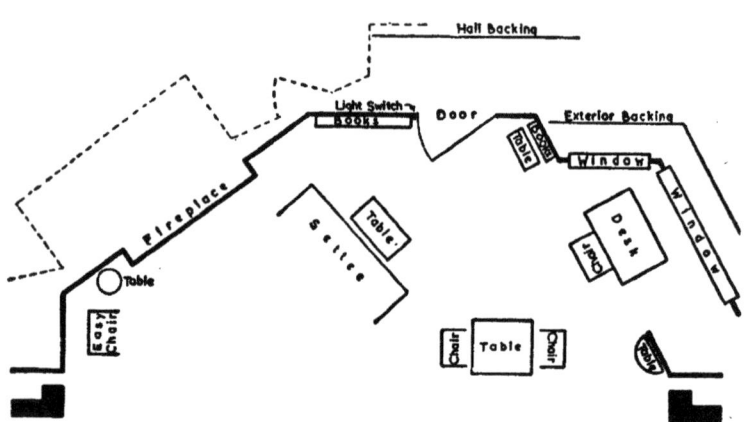

On stage.—Settee. *On it:* cushions
    Desk. *On it:* inkstand, blotter, papers, books, ashtray, matches, pamphlet, reading lamp
    Waste-paper basket
    Chair
    Table (*above settee*). *On it:* ashtray, matches, cigarette box
    Table (*up* L.). *On it:* whisky decanter, soda syphon, 2 glasses
    Table (*down* L.). *On it:* telephone, cigarette box, ashtray
    Table (*down* R.). *On it:* lamp
    Easy chair
    Card table. *On it:* 2 exercise books, 2 pencils, 3 school books
        On the floor beside it: book, satchel
    On the mantelpiece: cigarette box, ashtray, matches, clock, ornaments
    Vases of flowers
    Books

Off stage R.—Tray. *On it:* coffee percolator, sugar basin, milk jug, 3 cups and saucers, 3 spoons (STEPHEN)
    LAURA'S coat (STEPHEN)

Off stage L.—Scarf (STEPHEN)

Personal.—STEPHEN: cigarette case, wrist-watch

At end of Scene Strike: tray, cups, folding chairs

SCENE 2

Set: book in easy chair
Personal.—MRS USHER: handbag, umbrella

68

THE DAY'S MISCHIEF   69

Scene 3

The Vinings' room

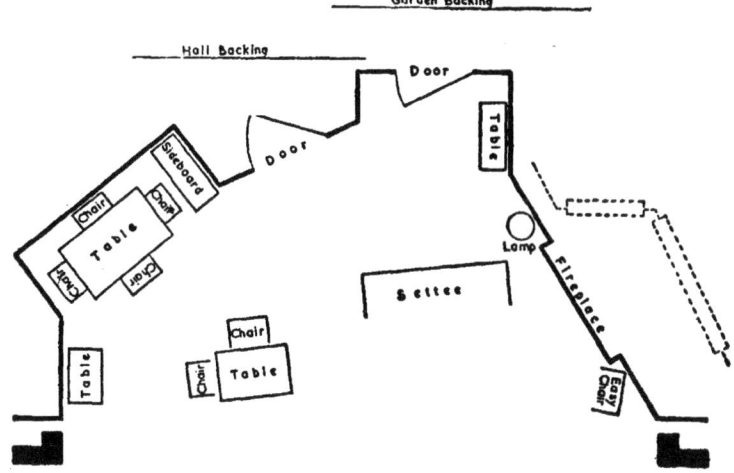

On stage.—Settee. *On it:* cushions
Dining table. *On it:* runner, bowl of flowers
Sideboard. *On it:* jug of water, dressing
Table (*down* R.). *On it:* telephone, bottle of whisky, soda syphon, 2 glasses
Table (R.C.). *On it:* packet of cigarettes, box of matches, ashtray, drawer containing—packet of photographs, pink leaflet, 2 packets of letters tied with tape, book wrapped in brown-paper jacket, purse, calendar, ointment jar, wallet, duster, 2 empty talcum-powder boxes, and other items to fill
6 chairs
Easy chair
Table (up L.)
Hanging bird-cage
Standard lamp
On the mantelpiece: clock, ornaments

Personal.—Stephen: hat
At end of Scene Strike: book from settee, drawer from table up L.

ACT II

Scene 1

The Barlows' room as Act I Scene 1

Set: Newspaper in easy chair, full ashtray on table behind settee
Off stage L.—Coat (Grace)
Personal.—Evelyn: handbag containing—cigarette case, lighter

Scene 2

The VININGS' room as Act I Scene 3

Set : work-basket, socks, darning materials on table R.C. Cover bird-cage
Off stage R.—Tray. *On it :* scrambled eggs on toast, knife and fork, pepper and salt, coffee-pot, cup and saucer, spoon (VI)
Tray. *On it :* 4 glasses (VI)
Jug of water (LAURA)

MUSIC USE NOTE

Licensees are solely responsible for obtaining formal written permission from copyright owners to use copyrighted music in the performance of this play and are strongly cautioned to do so. If no such permission is obtained by the licensee, then the licensee must use only original music that the licensee owns and controls. Licensees are solely responsible and liable for all music clearances and shall indemnify the copyright owners of the play(s) and their licensing agent, Samuel French, against any costs, expenses, losses and liabilities arising from the use of music by licensees. Please contact the appropriate music licensing authority in your territory for the rights to any incidental music.

IMPORTANT BILLING AND CREDIT REQUIREMENTS

If you have obtained performance rights to this title, please refer to your licensing agreement for important billing and credit requirements.

www.ingramcontent.com/pod-product-compliance
Ingram Content Group UK Ltd.
Pitfield, Milton Keynes, MK11 3LW, UK
UKHW021846210426
5322IPUK00022B/496